# OWN YOUR FUTURE

## Wisdom for Wealth and a Better Tomorrow

Grant D. Fairley & Michael H. Lanthier

Own Your Future
Widsom for Wealth and a Better Tomorrow
US Edition
By Grant D. Fairley & Michael H. Lanthier

First Edition

Copyright © 2013 by Silverwoods Publishing – A Division of McK Consulting Inc.

www.silverwoods-publishing.com

All rights reserved. No part of this book may be reproduced in any form or by any electronic or mechanical means, including information storage and retrieval systems, without permission in writing from the publisher, except by a reviewer who may quote brief passages in a review.

Published by: Silverwoods Publishing – a division of McK Consulting Inc.
Toronto - Chicago

ISBN-13: 978-1481917940
ISBN-10: 1481917943

All rights reserved.

Cover design by Artists Tree
Cover photo - Paha_L/bigstock.com

Printed in the United States of America

Silverwoods Publishing

# DEDICATION

**Grant dedicates this book to:**

"My Scottish ancestors: the Fairleys, Cowans, Raes, Woods, et al., who passed on the traits of finding value, taking risks, being persistent and the love of invention." (To other cultural traditions, read here "thrifty," "ambitious," "stubborn" and "wacky.")

**Mike dedicates this book to**

"My father, Elmer Harold Lanthier, who showed me how to live my life well and how to make a difference through the wise use of money."

# TABLE OF CONTENTS

Dedication ................................................................................ iii
Acknowledgments ................................................................. vii
Note to the Reader ................................................................... x
Introduction ............................................................................ xi
Madness ................................................................................... 1
The Wise ................................................................................... 4
The Wealthy ............................................................................. 6
A Valuable Life ......................................................................... 8
S-S-S Not S-O-S ..................................................................... 11
Pass It On ............................................................................... 14
Conservation ......................................................................... 16
The Best of Times and the Worst of Times ......................... 19
People, Places and Things .................................................... 21
Cold Feet vs. Happy Feet ...................................................... 23
Being Broke vs. Being Poor .................................................. 25
Professionally Speaking ....................................................... 28
Small Words .......................................................................... 30
Will Power ............................................................................. 35
Accounting for Taste ............................................................ 38
Climate vs. Weather ............................................................. 41
It's A Small World After All .................................................. 44
Coping With a Crisis ............................................................. 47
Oil Changes ........................................................................... 50
Tick-Tock ............................................................................... 52
The Sage ................................................................................ 54

## TABLE OF CONTENTS

Learning to be Wealthy ............................................................. 56
In Good Company ...................................................................... 60
The Entrepreneur - The Good, the Bad and the Ugly ............................ 62
A Creative Touch ...................................................................... 71
Growing Up .............................................................................. 75
Family Style ............................................................................. 77
Having Fun ............................................................................... 80
Salud! ..................................................................................... 83
How Long Do You Have? ............................................................. 87
Stable vs. Safe ......................................................................... 89
Take It to the Bank ................................................................... 92
Rainy Days ............................................................................... 94
Insure to Be Sure ..................................................................... 96
Can I Borrow That? ................................................................... 99
Playing Cards .......................................................................... 102
The Keys ................................................................................ 104
Your Castle ............................................................................. 106
Protecting Your Castle .............................................................. 108
Buying a Castle ....................................................................... 110
Improving Your Castle .............................................................. 112
Selling Your Castle .................................................................. 115
Castles by the Sea .................................................................. 117
Castles for Rent ...................................................................... 120
Taking Stock ........................................................................... 122
Bonding ................................................................................. 124
The Feeling Is Mutual .............................................................. 126
Courage ................................................................................. 129
Burst! ................................................................................... 132
When They Come Knocking ...................................................... 134
Humble Pie ............................................................................ 137
It's Only Money ...................................................................... 139
A Platinum Retirement ............................................................. 141
Continuing Education ............................................................... 146
Multiply ................................................................................. 149
Useful Links and Contacts ........................................................ 153
About the Authors ................................................................... 157

# ACKNOWLEDGMENTS

## From Grant

I would like to acknowledge the many people who have guided me through the many life experiences that have taught me not just about the financial world but how to value the important intangibles of life like our spiritual life, our relationships and our hope.

Ted Roberts and Ross Downing have always provided me with important financial insights. David E. Johnson has been invaluable in understanding the many nuances of the insurance world.

There are a host of other financial commentators, writers and speakers who have had an impact on my thinking over the many years of being interested in this subject. One who is still missed is the legendary Louis Rukeyser, who would enchant generations with his unique perspectives on the world of investing through his show, *Wall Street with Louis Rukeyser*. His many guests were always interesting and informative. We have the benefit of so many sources of real-time financial reporting on CNBC and Bloomberg in the USA and BNN in Canada. *The Economist* and *Bloomberg's Businessweek* magazines are read enthusiastically as they arrive each week.

My grandfather, James A. Cowan, was someone who moved in a wide range of financial and corporate circles in Canada and around the world in his role in public relations. As Canada's first public relations specialist, he innovated new ways of thinking about and doing business. My many discussions with him created an interest for me at an early age to understand the business world.

My great-uncle, Stuart Cowan, was a writer for the Canada's Globe & Mail newspaper financial section. As a teenager, I enjoyed talking with him about the world of finance.

## From Mike

I would like to thank my wife, Michelle, for her love and encouragement over our life together. She is a wonderful partner in our many business adventures and in this project as well.

My father and mother gave me the solid foundation of loving home where we children were valued and where my parents modeled their love for each other. This was a great gift for all of us. Dad was a veteran of World War II and set a great example for us. I miss them both very much every day.

As an entrepreneur, my father showed us the value of honesty and customer service for any business. He created Harcote in 1968 that served companies in the Fortune 500 as well as smaller local businesses. No matter what size the customer was, all were treated with a commitment to excellence in the products and services Harcote provided. Dad was also someone with a gift for finance and investment. He showed me many important concepts of how the investment world worked. That became a passion for me as well.

Many other friends and family have continued to be part of my story. For all of them, I am grateful.

Our faith has also been a sustaining strength over the course of our lives as we have faced the ups and downs along the way that is part of life today.

I also want to acknowledge the many positive colleagues and business relationships that have been part of my career. I have learned a great deal from others along the way.

## Together

On our life's journey, we have endeavored to learn from the wise people we would meet, hear or read. We are grateful for the many wise men and women who have influenced our thinking and our lives. We trust that the bits of wisdom you might find in here that we have received and now pass along will be useful to you as well.

Special thanks goes to our editors David Moadel and Daphne Parsekian, transcriptionist Jennifer Alvarez and Jeny Lyn Ruelo who did the layout.

# NOTE TO THE READER

Finances are like health. They are intensely personal topics. In medicine, there are things that are generally true but might require a different course of treatment for a particular individual with his or her unique factors of age, heredity and other conditions.

This is also true when you explore the world of money. This book will give you some of the insights and principles that are generally true for most people most of the time.

Good medical information usually includes the reminder to consult your healthcare professionals to see what is best for you.

This book is intended to share general financial information only. You should seek the advice of professionals before you make any investment or other financial decision based on the content of this book. Those professionals may include financial advisers, banking professionals, accounting and tax planners, lawyers, real estate professionals, investment advisers and others.

The author, publisher and anyone connected to this project assume no responsibility for any decisions, actions or outcomes from any of the content of this book, promotional information or other presentations related to this publication.

# INTRODUCTION

One of the most difficult areas for most people to discuss is money. This is in part because there are so many layers of thinking about personal finances. Perhaps only human sexuality rivals it as an uncomfortable area to discuss with even close friends and family members.

There are a number of reasons for this. One is that financial decisions (past, present and future) reflect a great deal about who we are as people and what we value. How much of my income will be saved vs. spent vs. shared? Am I someone who is more concerned about today or tomorrow? What does it say about me if I spend – a spendthrift? What does it say about me if I save – a miser?

Our culture is filled with many stories and tales that give us different views of how people deal with their money. Another of the reasons is that money or the absence of it is used as a measure of our standing in society. People with money are often treated as more valuable to society than those who have less. These kinds of status measures make people reluctant to discuss whether they have more or less money. If you have less money, you will be reluctant to admit that in case people think less of you. If you have more money, you may be concerned that people will resent your wealth.

A third reason is that we are never formally taught about personal finances in a way that is both meaningful and useful. This makes people depend on what little they have heard from others or what might be on a late-night paid programming series on how to get rich in ten steps. You do not have to be very old before you feel embarrassed to admit that you just do not know much about it. Another reason is that like many taboo topics, this is an area with a great deal of jargon. This keeps the experts in control, as it excludes those who do not know all of the secret passwords and keywords.

Finally, it will come as a surprise to many people that money is first and foremost an emotional topic rather than a factual one. That is one of the reasons that money can lead to arguments, stress and painful life experiences. Notice that we did not say that a lack of money causes those negative feelings, as many people who are very wealthy experience the same emotional traumas.

*Own Your Future* is one of the seminars we do with Strategic Seminars and our related seminar services. The principles are also included in our executive coaching work where needed, as well. We wanted to make this available to a wider audience through this book. We trust that it will encourage and guide you on your wealth journey. Over the more than 25 years that Grant has been doing this kind of seminar, he has met many people who chase after money and end up with huge gaps in a true wealth portfolio.

In this book, we hope to deal with the emotional, values and factual perspectives to give you a fresh look at this topic that impacts so much of our life. We sincerely hope that this will help you to make better decisions with the money you have, as well as the money you will earn over your lifetime.

# MADNESS

One of the surprises that most people have at our seminars in which they learn about wealth is that first and foremost, money is an emotional topic.

If you never understand this, you will always be financially challenged no matter whether you are rich or poor or somewhere in between. This is a key concept that will unlock your future and perhaps explain many of your experiences up to now with your spending, saving and investing.

Think about it. What are the two "sentiments" of Wall Street or Bay Street? Commentators and financial reporters will speak about investors as being "bullish" or "bearish." As you may know, a bull market is one that is usually going up and a bear market is one that is usually going down. However, beneath those two great images is another pair of words that you do not hear quite as often. *Fear* and *greed* are also words that describe what is happening in the marketplace. Listen carefully and you will also hear those words – or words that mean that. The excesses of the stock market involve people being too greedy, as they believe that the market will only keep going up. Greed is what feeds and sustains a "bubble" until it bursts. On the other side, when the market is going down, investors are driven by fear, as they believe that it will only get worse. This causes them to stay away from opportunities that might be in the market to make money because they are afraid.

Madness!

Both extremes are a form of collective madness that regularly attracts the investing crowd to jump off of one cliff or another together. The worst part is that many investors never know that they are caught up in the emotional roller coaster because they are shown numbers that say things are going up or down. The presence of so much "information" about investments leads people to think that it is a matter of knowledge. Facts matter, but without the emotional awareness, you will never be able to succeed financially.

However, the emotional side of money does not just apply to the stock market. The feelings that we have about money can cause us to be impulsive in how we spend our money. We all know that advertisers target our emotions as much as they try to appeal to our mind that a certain purchase is a smart decision. So, whether you are in or out of the stock market or some other investment, you still need to understand that money is all about our emotions.

This is not to say that emotions are negative. We need our emotional side to be one of the guides for us in the decision-making process. If we do not know that emotions are not just present in our financial decisions but are one of the loudest voices we hear in our head, we are vulnerable to being fooled or being foolish.

Every few years we hear about another "Ponzi Scheme" in which someone has ripped off a large group of investors. The plan promises people an amazing return on their investment with no risk. Those who invest early are paid through investments of others who come in later. This continues with more and more people investing in this get-rich-quick plan that their friends are assuring them is sending them big payments as promised. Before long, people are begging to be included in the bonanza. Then at some point, there are no longer enough new investors to pay the earlier investors when their payments come due. Finally, the whole sham falls apart and people learn that there really was no investment – just a churning of new dollars. One of the more recent examples is the Madoff scandal in New York in which some sophisticated and wealthy people bought the lie. In the end, many individuals and organizations were defrauded of millions of dollars while the perpetrator skimmed off a king's ransom along the way.

Every time it happens, people treat it as some new idea of how to fleece the gullible people. But this scam has been around for a very long time. Its name came from Charles Ponzi when he used the sale of international postage stamps as the get-rich-quick strategy in the U.S. in 1920. For those who have read or seen the miniseries *Little Dorrit* by Charles Dickens, you know that the same kind of fraud was described in that novel in 1857. This is not a new thing. But neither is the greed that people have for a get-rich-quick scheme with no risks at all. High rewards and high risks go together, if they work out great. Low risks usually include low rewards. That we understand, too. But if someone tells you that there is a special deal for you that has high returns and no risk, tell them that you have read about *Little Dorrit*. Greed will blind even the otherwise sensible people if they are not careful.

So how can you be successful in your investments? How can you make good decisions with your spending? How do you know how much to put away for tomorrow vs. how much to spend today? Whom should you trust for financial advice? Where does it all begin?

Do not be fearful. Do not be greedy.

What's left?

Be wise.

# THE WISE

There are many books about learning to become a wise person. Most of them are quite ancient. We do not talk about being wise much anymore. If there ever were an area of life in which wisdom is essential, it is money. So let us do a quick review of what it means to be wise.

If you study what is said about wise people or how to become one, you learn that wisdom includes many different concepts. In wisdom, you will find knowledge, understanding, experience, confidence, peace and strength, as well as many other characteristics. The most optimistic part of the wisdom topic is that you can grow in wisdom. That is hopeful for all of us! To be sure, wisdom is a journey. Wisdom is also something that can be shared. That is great because it means that we do not have to make all of the mistakes that are there to make before we can become wise.

Whom do you know that you would consider to be a wise woman or a wise man? That is different from knowing someone who is smart or talented or charismatic. What makes you think of someone as a wise person?

When would you like to talk to a wise person? If you are like most people, you want to speak to a wise woman or man when a big decision must be made. What is the best choice I can make? What will give me the best result?

Wisdom includes seeking advice. Presidents and prime ministers have counsellors to give them advice. In disputes between people, companies or groups, we go to court in the hope that a wise judge will help to settle the dispute. Ambassadors and negotiators work with countries in conflict to try to bring about positive changes and even peace. People who can consistently give useful advice and counsel are very valuable to a government, company or community.

As individuals, we benefit from the wise people in our lives. Perhaps it is a family member or friend who is the wise person you can trust to listen to you and give you sound advice. Personal counsellors, social workers, ministers and pastors often are there for us in this way.

Many people practice some form of financial counselling that offers you a range of services, including advice for your investments as well as financial planning. How do you choose a financial adviser who is best for you? Should I choose the one with the most expensive office, the priciest watch or the fastest car? Should I not follow success?

So why would I want to be wise if that did not guarantee that I would be rich?

Being rich is not the best target to have.

What is better than being rich?

The wise person would tell you – being wealthy.

# THE WEALTHY

So what is wrong with being rich? It is not good enough! You deserve better than that.

What does it mean to be wealthy? How is that different than being rich? Why should you aspire to be wealthy rather than just rich?

Let us go back to our wisdom idea again.

What do you imagine it would be like to be rich – if you are not already?

Here is a typical list:

- You would never have to work again.
- You could buy anything you want.
- You could go anywhere you want.
- You would not have to worry about anything again.

Of course, you have seen enough about rich people who have their lives lived out on the tabloids or courtrooms to know that it is not quite that easy. Follow the lives of those who won big money in a lottery, and you find that most either are broke again before long or very unhappy. Read the biographies of those who could buy anything, go anywhere and never have to work, and you will find that their lives are unfulfilled. Being able to quit your job and never work again sounds very appealing, especially if your job is a tough one. If it was only about being rich, you would not find any unhappy or unsatisfied rich people. Instead, you can find people who are wealthy with vast sums of money and others who are wealthy with very little. How is that possible? It depends on what you understand about what it means to be wealthy.

How rich you are is a measure of your assets minus your liabilities.

How wealthy you are is a measure of the quality of your life.

Your quality of life goes way beyond the arithmetic of your personal finances. It includes your values as a person and your understanding of what is fulfilling in life. Riches by themselves are a trap. That is why you need to sort out who you are as a person before you concentrate on how to build and expand your personal fortune. If you are able to do this, then no matter what your bank account may say today, you will find life worth living. We all learn that if we chase happiness, we never really find it. True happiness finds us when we are living life well. It is the same thing with true wealth. When we make choices that position us to have meaningful lives, we find that we are open to better opportunities that can lead to lives that are rewarding and rewarded.

Skip this step, and what we cover in the rest of this book can make you rich. But you will have missed the better option of being wealthy.

Do not settle for being rich.

# A VALUABLE LIFE

It is one of the classics of the holiday season shown over and over again featuring Jimmy Stewart as the character George Bailey. George has spent his life serving the community and postponing his dreams of school, travel and building great buildings. During a financial crisis, he despairs and wishes that he had never been born. A heavenly ambassador helps George see what difference he has made in the lives of others by seeing all that would have been different had he not been born. That sets the stage for a happy ending in which George realizes that he truly has *A Wonderful Life*.

What is less obvious as you watch the movie is how much it is a different George as he travels through the altered life in which he was never had been born. George was cynical, angry, depressed and eventually desperate as he realized that he had never lived. What was truly heartbreaking for him was the loss of the relationships that mattered most to him. His younger brother died as a boy. His mother did not know him. His wife in his other life now thought that he was deranged, fearing him as a stalker. His children were never born. After wanting to "live again," George had no fear of the bank examiner, Mr. Potter, the police or even jail. He had discovered that he was truly wealthy no matter what his bank account might suggest.

What are your values? What do you consider to be your purpose in life? What makes you who you are? What relationships do you value the most? Where do you make a difference in your world as it is now?

Many people falsely believe that they would make a difference in the lives of others if they had money. The reality is that you will carry your values with you whether you are rich or poor. People who have no time to help others when they are poor seldom start being generous with their time once they have more money. We tend to become even more of what we are as we grow older. We also tend to become more of what we are when you add more dollars to our bank account. That is why our values and our character matter today.

One of the reasons why many rich people are not happy is because of how money can change relationships. Someone who is rich or someone who is very beautiful or especially talented in entertainment or sports now has to doubt his or her relationships. Does this person truly want to be my friend, or is it because I am rich (or good-looking or famous)? That doubt undermines the essential element of any successful relationship – trust. Do they like me as a person, or do they just want my money? What are they after? Why are they here? This leads to very few relationships that can be truly trusted and enjoyed. No wonder these people speak longingly about those relationships that they had before they became rich or famous. Those old friendships become the only ones they can really trust because they cared for them as they were without the power or money or celebrity.

So as part of your thinking about wealth, include on your balance sheet the relationships that you already have. Who are the friends and family who have always been there for you? Who are the people who have invested their time, attention and care in your life that have helped you get where you are today? What relationships in your life need attention? Are there relationships that could be healed by your willingness to forgive? Are there relationships that would be strengthened by a phone call or a visit? With all of the inexpensive tools of communication we now have in our world, people spend less time really sharing and caring than before. Posting a note on Facebook or tweeting on Twitter is a great group solution, but deep relationships are built one at a time.

Too late do many people realize that the relationships they will miss the most have not received the attention they should while the person is still around. Age, disease, accidents and moves can take people away from us very suddenly. Make sure that your relationships are up to date. We have to be intentional about this. It will not happen just because we acknowledge we should make that call or write that note. We have to plan to do it, or it too will slip away.

This is so important because when it comes to money, you will need a clear perspective. When we lack healthy relationships or our relationships are strained, the emotional turmoil that this will create can distract us from making wise decisions.

Make a list of your best friends. Make a list of people who could become one of your close friends. What do you need to do to make your friendships solid? Who are the family members that would benefit from a call or a visit?

Choose to build those relationships.

# S-S-S NOT S-O-S

Simple ways of thinking about complex subjects might sound like a bad idea unless the simplicity leads to clearer understanding and better choices. It is easy in the subject of finance to become overwhelmed by all of the jargon used in financial reporting and even in presentations that try to make investing easy.

One of the roles of an effective teacher is to boil down the large volume of information to give the student something he or she can actually use. Great teachers even make the flavour better, just like boiling down maple tree sap to sweet maple syrup. If the teacher has done this well, then you will want to learn more, with the benefit of the simple beginning leading you to the more complex ideas.

So what are the three S words that can be helpful here?

Save. Spend. Share.

These are the three big ideas that are part of a balanced approach to our money. Anyone who wants to make progress financially needs to understand and be intentional with these three practices.

"Save" covers the big ideas of saving and investing our money. This is how we make choices today to have more flexibility tomorrow. We decide to put some of our money to work for us in the future with the hope that it can become a financial partner for us later. We may continue to work years from now, but money that has been saved and invested wisely will be there to keep working too, generating income for us to help pay our bills and live more comfortably. If we arrive at the point where we no longer choose to work or can no longer work, money saved and invested well can help us to live on in addition to whatever government programs may or may not be there. We must choose to "save" for this to happen. Where and how we make those saving decisions will come later. But a good financial plan must include the balance of saving for the future.

"Spending" is something that many people do not need to practice – they are already experts! Most of us know how to spend. But spending wisely can be a way to ensure that we get the most out of our spending. That does not mean that we cannot have fun with our money. We do not need to feel guilty for enjoying "the fruits of our labour." Many people end up spending almost unconsciously. Money just seems to disappear and if asked, they really cannot tell you where it all went. We will discuss later some of the key ideas to spending well as part of living well. But make no mistake about it – we do spend our money.

"Share" might seem to be one of those words that should have an asterisk beside it. Why should we share our money? We worked hard for that money. We earned it. If someone does not have enough money, let them go earn some of their own. I pay taxes. Let the government take care of them. Sharing your money is not about others – it is about you. For you to choose to share with someone in need is something that changes you. In a strange way, it serves like an inoculation against becoming too greedy and obsessed with money. It helps you on the path to being a wealthy person rather than someone who happens to be rich. Sharing through your religious organization, your community groups or other charities is an investment in the world around you. Many cultures have a great divide between the wealthy and the poor. The rich are forever worrying about their safety and security because of the intense, angry poverty around them. They end up living in armed compounds without the freedom that you can enjoy in a balanced democracy in which we invest in each other. So decide to have some money to invest in those in need. It will do you a world of good!

Save. Spend. Share. Can it really be that simple? Yes, it starts there. Even after all of the sophisticated planning and investing have been done, if that simple balance does not exist in our lives, we will have missed out on so much in life that we might have enjoyed.

# PASS IT ON

One of the great gifts we can give to our children is to share ourselves with them. That includes our time, our energy, our support – and our knowledge. If we have graduated to the level of wisdom, then our children will be fortunate indeed to have us as parents.

As any parent knows, we will not fool our children by being someone we are not. They will value our honesty and our love for them – even when it drives them nuts. If we can share the big ideas of what we have learned and are learning financially, this is a great gift to pass on to the next generation. It helps to keep to the big ideas – like our chapter on the three S words. That is something that even young children can understand and participate in for themselves. Creating opportunities to develop positive habits will help them own the concepts for themselves. Seeing how we deal with questions of money will model for them in a powerful way.

Some of this is, of course, age-appropriate. Part of this is to not put on children the burdens intended for adults. Children should not be worrying about how to make the mortgage payment. But children can be part of being good stewards by not wasting the resources that have been purchased for the family.

It is helpful to share with our older children not just our successes but also some of our mistakes. That teaches them the reality that mistakes will be made. It then assures them that as they too make a mistake, they can move forward.

Children who receive a positive and balanced view of finances are more likely to approach the challenges of their finances with confidence when it comes time for them to make decisions. The conversations and other ways you include them in thinking about the way to understand money and its place in life is an investment in their future.

When children learn that money and all that is associated with it is only a means to an end and not an end in itself, you have shared wisdom with them. This saved them from an emptiness that you will find in people who have bought into the illusion that money brings happiness. Money makes a good servant but a terrible master.

Teaching this to our children early is an important part of being a great parent.

# CONSERVATION

One of the measures of financial progress is to know not just how much we earn or even how much we keep. How much do we save vs. how much we spend is the teeter-totter that can make or break a person's future wealth. Spending too much and saving too little will lead to a life that works for now but is a disaster later. Spending too little now and saving too much (Yes, you can do this!) can lead to a life that has all of the joy of Ebenezer Scrooge before that Christmas redemption.

The balance is to live well today *and* live well in the future.

Dollars saved today are the army of workers who will work for you in the future, if they are invested wisely. Dollars spent today are important for you and your family to have a balanced life in the short time that you can make a difference for them. As older parents will tell you, they grow up too fast. As the classic song "The Cats and The Cradle" warns us, if we miss out on their childhood years, you will never get those back. Just as importantly, you may not have the quality of relationship that will make your older years meaningful.

So how do you balance the two? How do you know how much to save? How much should you spend? (Sharing is another of the 3 "S" words that will be covered later.)

Some people are enthusiastic "budgeteers." They love to create a budget and then measure themselves against the expected income and expenses. Other people are like those who react to the word "diet" by immediately developing a craving to eat even more.

If you are one of those people who thrive on a budget as part of your financial planning – use it! Remember that your budget is measuring your future expectations and goals. Once you start the actual process of spending and saving within your budget, you will quickly find that some of your best estimates were wrong. That is okay as long as you are careful to find some additional income or reduce your expenses elsewhere to keep your overall budget on track.

What if you are one of the many people who cannot work with or within a budget? Some say it is the math. Others say that they do not enjoy the accounting. Some are spontaneous spenders who do not want the pressure and accountability of setting and keeping to a budget. Then there are those who have wildly variable incomes or expenses because of the type of job or lifestyle that they have. If you do not work from a budget, the price you must pay is to be more conservative on your saving and rainy day funds. Instead of having a savings account with the equivalent of three months of income, you need to set aside the income for six months.

An important ingredient for financial health is the ability to slow spending when things get tough. That assumes that you have room to slow your spending. Some people end up with fixed costs that cannot be reduced and which allow no flexibility to cut spending. If you are spending every dollar on your mortgage, taxes, heating, insurance and other necessities, it is only a matter of time until you will face a financial crack. If your situation is too tense and too tight, you will not have the flexibility to spend a little more or a little less as your life will require. This usually happens because people buy too much house (or rent too much condominium) with the hope that they will end up further ahead sooner. This may sound good in theory, but sooner or later you will have an "event horizon" in which you need additional money to make everything work to stay stable. Not an emergency that would require the rainy day funds – this might be a bump in fuel costs or taxes or especially interest rates. Suddenly you need to have more money available each month. The choice then becomes an extra job or a cut in spending.

There are good reasons why lenders like a bank will review your financial position and use ratios of what percentage of your income is being used to service debt. If you are above those ratios, you are at risk that everything could collapse. It is better to build in some flexibility to your spending as a strategy to conserve your assets so that they can grow.

The other key concept about conserving your future is to buy quality at a good price. Both of these ingredients are necessary. Some people buy quality but overpay for it. Eventually that may work itself out, but it is usually unnecessary. Others will get a great price, but what they are buying is not of good quality. It is only a matter of time (usually a short time) before the purchase turns sour since it no longer serves its purpose. It does not last or satisfy because it was not of good value.

How do you make this work? Most items of value go through phases when they are more or less expensive. Buy the best value you can afford when the prices are down. That is the best of both worlds. You will conserve your future by reducing waste and disappointment.

# THE BEST OF TIMES AND THE WORST OF TIMES

Along the journey of life, we have our best view looking backward. So many of the highs and lows of our life only make sense with the perspective of time and age. There is a reason why people in their fifties and beyond have a better sense of who they are and what life is all about. There is a reason why people in their seventies and beyond tell so many stories. They have them – and they know which ones matter.

Here are some of the big ideas that each of us needs to embrace.

## Prepare for success.

In the early days of ecommerce on the internet, one of the terrors for many new ventures would be what to do if they suddenly were successful! Unlike the traditional sales-inventory-fulfillment chains of the traditional business, the world wide web created the possibility that many orders could be transmitted instantly from anywhere in the world. What if you had more orders than products to fill those orders? The other scenario was creating a website that was so popular that it would time-out or even crash due to all the people trying to access it at the same time. This all created the need for "scalability" where you could adjust your product supply or bandwidth to accommodate success.

This is true for all of us. Think about anything you have as a passion, a dream or even just a project in your life. What if that part of your life suddenly turned into a huge success? Success is something that many wish for but few actually plan to encounter. The more you can plan for success, the more likely you are to be able to translate that success into future opportunities for the long term.

## Prepare for failure.

Just as we often do not prepare adequately to succeed, many of us do not prepare for failure. To certain elements of the successful thinking movements, to consider failure is to create it. You must never admit that failure is possible, or you will bring it onto yourself.

However, many successful people will tell you that it was easier for them to go out and face the challenges of being successful because they had thought through what would happen in this project or that one had failed. Planning what you would do when business or life does not turn out as planned is actually a good strategy for long-term success.

As you learn from reading the biographies of many successful people in various areas of life, they often encountered failure, learned from it and moved forward. Others who are surprised by failure often find it difficult to deal with disappointment when failure strikes. Those kinds of exercises can be very useful for everyone.

Like a good fire drill, knowing where to go and what to do in an emergency may become a life-or-death decision.

Like a good sports practice, the experience of scoring in practice helps you prepare to make the moves and decisions that make it more likely that you will score in the big game.

# PEOPLE, PLACES AND THINGS

In the quest to know who we are, it is helpful to understand what we value. This is a bit different from our "values" in the sense of our moral compass or code. In this case, the question is designed to help us identify how we sort out our commitment to people, places and things.

Some individuals value their relationships above all else. If their relationships are going well, they have a greater sense of well-being, too. They measure their wealth in part through their friendships and their family relationships. The more deeply felt and cultivated relationships that they can identify, the healthier they feel as human beings.

Others are very attached to places. This could be their family home. It might extend to a family cottage, farm or ranch that is part of their story. They know the land, the trees, and the lake, and in being there, they find some of their identity as a sense of wholeness. Places can also include a special travel destination or even the joy of traveling to more and more new places to add to their collection. Often though they also join Dorothy in *The Wizard of Oz* when she announced at the end of the movie that "There's no place like home."

Other people love collecting "things" as part of their well-being. It might be stamps, coins, Royal Doulton figurines or paintings by a particular artist. The focus on the care and accumulation of these things is very important to them. Where they live, whether or not they travel and whom they spend time with in their relationships become less of a focus.

Of course, many people value a combination of people, places and things. Understanding what type of person you and those around you are will help you make better financial decisions together. If you ignore this area, you can end up with a partner who does not have as part of his or her story with you what is very important to him or her. If you are both "people people," then it is easy to concentrate your time and investments on the people in your life. If you are both "places people," then those shared trips and vacations will fill your memories with shared experiences to relive together. If you are "things people," then you can enjoy the collections of things you accumulate over time.

However, if you are a different type than your partner, make sure that both of you are adding to the list of important people, places and things in your life. Beyond your spouse, you may also find that your children are different than you are. Some parents who love to travel find that one or more of their children are homebodies who prefer to spend time with their friends or collections. Try to be aware and sensitive to those differences within the family. As is true in so much of family life, the differences within the family can enrich as well as annoy us. That is what it means to be in a family.

# COLD FEET VS. HAPPY FEET

If you are someone who makes decisions easily and well, feel free to skip on to the next chapter. This chapter is not for those who are decisive and who regularly make great decisions. Those are the people with "happy feet" who are always ready to move forward, backward, or sideways or jump in the air as needed. They trust their judgment and move on.

Others face decisions with fear. As with so much in life, fear can immobilize you. Your concern about making the very best decision can act like a fog that rolls in and covers all of the possible decisions that you might make. Suddenly you are not sure what you should do.

After agonizing for a very long time and working through the system you have developed to make a decision, you still find yourself hesitating. You do not have "happy feet" – you have "cold feet." We often think of cold feet when it comes to a big decision like getting married or following through on a decision to make a major purchase. What seemed like a sure thing now seems uncertain. All of the doubts begin to chew away at your self-confidence that you have made a great choice.

The reference to cold feet is associated with our sense of fear or danger. In a crisis, the blood naturally goes to our vital organs to ensure our ability to survive. The extremities become cold. If what we are facing is particularly difficult, we may go into shock. Shivering is another way the body automatically reacts to a crisis like a dangerous cold. Fainting is another of the body's reactions to danger or extreme surprise. Cold feet in most people is a sign of stress. As it does not feel "right," it can cause us to hesitate and ultimately freeze in our ability to make a positive decision.

This is not always a bad thing. In fact, changing our mind is not a sign of weakness if we discover that we are on the wrong track. If, however, it is not the facts that have changed but just your confidence, then you need to warm up those feet.

People with cold feet often confuse certainty with assurance. Certainty is knowing without a doubt that there is only one wise and successful course of action. Very few things in life can have that kind of certainty. *Assurance* is a better term for us to understand. Assurance comes from a careful review of the situation and the alternatives that you can discover. Often it also involves asking other professionals or trusted family members or friends for their input, as well. Assurance comes when you understand that you have as much information as you can reasonably find and you choose to act on the best decision you can make.

Does that mean that these decisions will be perfect? Of course not. However, you will make decisions wise enough to encourage your confidence in the future decisions you will face. That is a great way to warm up those cold feet into happy feet.

# BEING BROKE VS. BEING POOR

It may seem like the same thing. I am broke. I am poor. But the difference is a world apart.

Being broke is a calculation of your cash flow – you have no money.

Being poor is a miscalculation of your assets.

What I mean by that is that many people are broke from time to time. For some, it was when they were starting out with nothing in the bank and living from moment to moment. Others "went broke" after a calamity like a business that failed, a health problem, a divorce or through long-term unemployment.

In fact, many of the most successful people have been broke at different points in their lives. We love to hear the rags-to-riches stories of people who had nothing but worked hard until they were able to make a good living for themselves and their families. We all appreciate those generations who sacrificed to give their children a chance to have a better life than they did through education and opportunity. For those who start a business, there is a high degree of risk and many new businesses will fail. Many talented and ultimately successful people like Walt Disney knew what it was like to go bankrupt and have to start again. Eventually, their persistence paid off.

Being poor is a state of mind and heart. We can use "poorer" and "richer" in a comparative sense that someone is wealthier or less wealthy than someone else. That is different that being poor. The great tragedy of unemployment and generational poverty is that it can take away the dignity and sense of value that comes from work. Work is in our DNA. When people no longer work, many changes begin to occur that rob them of their sense of self and purpose. This is why it is in society's best interest to have high levels of employment and low levels of unemployment. Unemployment rots communities. Like a disease, unhealthy communities rarely stay confined to where they begin – they spread and infect the lives of others. This is why the answer to the age-old question about being my brother's keeper has to be, "Yes!" There will always be those in our society who through health problems, mental illness, accidents, advancing age, the elderly and other life traumas who will need our support. Taking care of those who cannot care for themselves is not just charity – it is an investment. For those who are capable of more, we can encourage them toward finding a better tomorrow. We live in a time in which technology is eliminating types of work done for generations. There are large waves of the unemployed who will never have the same job waiting for them to return. They do not have the education or skills to move into areas where the jobs are. Further challenges come to Western countries as the rise of new labour markets in countries like China and India invite competition for jobs in places where the cost of living is very different from the West. These are huge challenges.

This challenge cannot be met until we agree on the opportunity and risk as a community in which there is long-term unemployment. Communities that do not continue to restructure and adapt so that people can find and keep meaningful work are damaging the human infrastructure that keeps a society moving forward.

For those who believe that they are "poor," we have to take their view off their cash-flow report and turn them to their assets and liability statement. We all have great assets.

These begin with our value as people. Rich or poor – all people are of equal value. Each of us has different gifts, abilities and experiences. For some, these may be well recognized and developed. For others, these may not be identified and may not have been exercised as they might be. That is why opportunity is so important. Giving people the opportunity to explore who they are, what they care about and what they are good at doing early on is one of the great gifts of education. Primary and secondary education should help us on that quest to explore our world and ourselves while giving us the basic tools we will need to take advantage of opportunities in our future.

We have the asset of our personality. If we are someone who is willing to work hard, that is a very valuable asset. Are we someone who likes to help others? That's gold. Do we have some special skill or interest that could be developed? There are many ways to add up our list of assets.

Turning poverty around begins with enabling the person who is broke to see a way out of his poverty. That includes giving him the tools and opportunities to move forward as he is willing to do so.

As anyone who knows both the wealthy and those of modest means will tell you, some of the happiest people do not have large bank accounts. Some of those who seem to have everything are indeed very poor when it comes to what makes life worth living.

So if you are one of those struggling today without two pennies to rub together, do not give up – you are just broke. Believe in your tomorrows and work hard to seize any of the opportunities you can find to move forward. You can do it!

# PROFESSIONALLY SPEAKING

There are places and times when it is wise to receive professional advice. We all benefit from being under the regular care of physicians both to recover from health problems and, more importantly, to prevent them. If we encounter difficulties in our life experiences, a professional counsellor can be a great help. During times of spiritual stress or pain, seeking a spiritual adviser from your faith community can help.

There are financial advisers that we use, as well. Some are directly involved in our finances, such as investment consultants, financial advisers and investment brokers. We also have access to advisers from our banks.

Then there are the second-line but just as important professionals. Bookkeepers help us track our activity. Accountants help us to plan our taxes. Real estate advisers work with us during the sale or purchase of a house. Lawyers assist us in estate planning and legal transactions, and when we encounter legal problems.

The first rule is: You are in charge of your life and business. No one can or will care as much about your future as you do. Never hand over an area of your life or finances and assume it is the professional's responsibility for all to go well. They are part of your financial team. You are still the general manager who must make it all work, hold others accountable and take responsibility for the decisions that are made.

The second rule is: When you need advice, buy the best advice you can afford. Do not miss the first part of this rule. You need to know when to seek advice. When you do need advice, get the greatest expertise that you can actually afford to use. This might seem unfair since someone with more money may have better access to the top advisers than you do. Get over it. Then look for ways to access better advice with the budget you have available.

# SMALL WORDS

Many of the words that are most important are short words. Love. Life. Child. Mom. Dad. Faith. Hope.

This is true in the financial world, as well. It is like medicine and law in that it has its own language with many strange terms that are closer to the ancient languages of Greek and Latin from where they originate than to the English we speak today. One of those short words that have a huge impact on our financial life is "tax."

People often have no idea how much tax they pay. Part of this is due to many taxes being hidden within purchases or called "fees" or camouflaged in a variety of other ways.

So, what is a tax?

A tax is when you pay a government directly or indirectly. Direct taxation happens when we have deductions for income tax taken from our paycheque. It also happens when we have a property tax bill to pay. Many other indirect taxes are collected by businesses when we make a purchase, as in a sales tax or value-added tax. Taxes may be income based – you pay a higher rate of tax when you earn more (also known as a progressive tax.) Some taxes are a flat, with the same rate no matter how much you earn or spend. Some income taxes are structured this way, but more often that is how a sales tax works. The more you spend, the more tax you will spend, but it will always be at 5% or 13% or whatever the rate is. Less obvious are the taxes that are rolled into our purchases, as when we fill our gas tank. Not only are there sales taxes there, but also royalties and other forms of taxation in every litre or gallon we pump.

Investments may be subject to taxes. Interest investments like a savings account or money market fund (largely made of government treasury bills and some corporate short-term debt) are subject to the highest rate of taxation, counting most of the time like our paycheque earnings. Depending on the country and its current rules, there is often an advantage given to those who earn their money through dividends (money shared from profits to the shareholders who own the company.) A different rate is applied to those who sell their investment for a profit (known as a capital gain) in something like a stock or piece of real estate. Some investments like owning your home have special tax considerations that currently either allow deductions on the interest portion of your mortgage in the United States or no tax on the increase in value when you sell your home in the case of Canada. Both are a tax benefit but in different ways.

Governments (and the industries and groups that lobby for special rules) will allow you to have extra deductions or tax credits if you choose to use your money in ways that they wish you to do so. An example of that is the tax credit you receive for donating to charities. Here, the government recognizes that charities provide services and play a role that is beneficial for society. Rewarding those who donate to these religious and not-for-profit social organizations is a way to ensure that they can afford to function and benefit the community. A tax break given toward saving for your retirement, as another example, recognizes that money saved will create more wealth and independence later (and they will catch up on those taxes when you finally retrieve money from that larger pot later!)

So what is a tax really all about? A tax is the money that citizens and companies give to governments to function. Whatever a government does is paid for by taxes collected somewhere. (When the money reaches the government, it has a metamorphosis. It is no longer called a tax – it is now called revenue. That sounds better now, does it not?)

Some people would have you believe that all taxes are bad. Others will act as if there is never enough money for government – it should receive much more (of someone else's) money to do even more. The pendulum of higher and lower taxes swings over the decades and in different ways in different countries.

Before discussing taxes, there is an earlier question to discuss. What kind of society do we want to have? What are the elements of our civilization that give us the ability to live with the freedoms and peace that our government should facilitate for us? We want the safety of police, fire and emergency services.

What about education? Is society a better place for all of us if we have children who can read, write and function successfully in the workplace and the community?

What about healthcare? Is it in society's best interest to have people who are healthy? When someone is ill, is it better for society to be able to care for him or her in hospital? Do children with special needs, adults who are injured and unable to work or the elderly need the care of society? What if society did not provide for those who could not care for themselves? What about the poor or long-term unemployed? What kind of society would you have then?

But what if some of these "social safety nets" undermine personal responsibility and then take away any incentive for a person to provide for themselves or their family?

These are the two ends of the spectrum that face governments and their people everywhere. How much should we do? How much can we afford to do? How many tax dollars can we raise to accomplish these projects? At what point do you take so many taxes out of the economy that the people working and earning the money no longer have the incentive to work? What is the distance between our society as it is and life in other countries, in which the wealthy live in guarded compounds living in fear that they or their children will be held for ransom?

How much of a balanced, peaceful life can we afford to enjoy as a civilized society?

The follow-up to that is then, what taxes need to be collected to ensure that government can provide?

The next question is what kinds of taxes provide the money without damaging the economy that generates these revenues?

Finally, we have to hold governments at all levels accountable for the quality and results of their spending, just as you would evaluate anyone who was doing a job for you.

So how do we handle taxes on a personal level? Pay the taxes you owe as you owe them, and do not support the underground economy in which people do not report their income to avoid paying the cost of society. That does not mean to overpay your taxes – use the professionals discussed later to pay your fair tax. But if you are doing things like supporting charities or other community activities through your gifts, there is nothing wrong with taking those deductions or credits to lower your tax bill.

For your investments, do not make investments because of the tax benefit. Always choose the best investment based on its fundamentals. Would you buy this investment if there were no tax benefits? If the answer is yes, then move forward with any tax breaks as a bonus. Many people have ended up investing for the tax breaks only to learn that they have lost their investment because the tax breaks were used to distract the investors from the poor-quality investment.

Taxes that are spent well by governments efficiently and effectively delivering the services a society desires and can afford are an investment. Anything else is a waste.

# WILL POWER

Just as insurance is important in facing uncertainties, there are legal decisions you need to make for the probability of infirmity and the certainty of death.

Death is a subject that people avoid as if you can keep death further away by not talking about it. Often it is questions of life and death that we would rather not discuss. For the sake of your loved ones, take the time to face planning your estate – meaning your instructions for your assets and liabilities after your death.

Many people assume that they do not need to have a will until they are wealthy or advanced in years. In fact, it is wise for every adult to have a will. This does not just make the legal issues clearer in the event of your death; it guides your loved ones on what your wishes and directions were.

While it is not required in many jurisdictions to have a lawyer create your will, it is a good idea to do so. Do you know the difference between the words "vague" and "ambiguous" if I were to ask? Words matter. They especially matter when it comes to the law and courts. Vague or ambiguous instructions in a will can force something that should be easy to have to be reviewed in a court to determine what you meant. One of the advantages of using a lawyer who does estate planning as part of his practice is that he has the training and the experience to help you word your instructions clearly. Also important is the long list of "what ifs" that you need to consider in case your first ideas no longer apply. A good lawyer will take you through the process so that you can express clearly what you would like to have done with your assets and possessions when you die. It is worth the investment.

One of the functions of creating your will is to appoint an executor(s) for your will. This person has the responsibility to carry out your instructions. Often he or she is a spouse or close family member. Sometimes she or he is a close friend with business experience who can follow through for you. I always recommend that you meet with your executor before he or she is appointed in your will to be sure that he is willing to serve. You also should go over with them the instructions so that they hear it from you. Often you will have alternative executors to serve if the original one you appointed is unable to serve when it is needed.

How do you divide your estate? Having watched many families in the period after losing a loved one, the pain can be compounded if a will is not in place or if it is poorly designed.

Subject to the laws of your jurisdiction, it is also an opportunity to provide some healing. Many wills have the opposite effect as they are used to settle scores or to stick the knife into an unfortunate relationship one more time. The trauma of an unexpected death can be made worse by a will that adds to the emotional turmoil. Harsh words or choices can leave a legacy of pain. Instead, it is wise to try to use the words that will be spoken on your behalf after you are gone to make a positive statement. If you can, try to treat your children or other relationships as "equitably" as possible. For some, that means an identical percentage of what is left. Sometimes you cannot be "identical" with the assets due to what they are. So in those cases, please be sure to be as balanced as you can be so that there is less reason for conflict at a time when they have just lost you.

If you have minor children (or adult children with special needs), you will need to appoint a guardian for them. This is the person or family with whom they would go to live if there were no longer a parent available to raise them. Once again, this needs to be carefully considered. Often a close family member will be appointed. Where no one from the family is available, it might be friends who take this responsibility. Once you have decided who you think would be able to raise your children with the values and opportunities that you would wish them to have, you need to discuss this with the potential guardian(s), too. Always ask their permission before making such an appointment. Not everyone is emotionally equipped to take on this important responsibility. Let them know some of the things that are important to you for your children, like valuing an education or developing their talents, for example. Be sure that you have done your life insurance and financial planning to provide enough money for the children's care so that they are not a burden on the guardian's family. In the end, you have to have confidence that the potential guardian will do his best for you and your children if you cannot continue in that role.

Living wills and powers of attorney are another topic to discuss with a lawyer. These become the sources of legal guidance for those caring for you if you are incapacitated by accident or illness. It is for those who love you to know what your preferences are about healthcare and property decisions if you can no longer make them for yourself.

# ACCOUNTING FOR TASTE

Accountants, bookkeepers and other tax advisers are very valuable. The largest annual expense for most people is not the cost of their housing or food or healthcare. It is their taxes.

As most taxes are deducted at the source, many people do not realize how many dollars are being paid in taxes. Instead, they focus on the amount of their refund. Do you know how many dollars you paid in various taxes last year? If not, you probably have not spent enough time planning with your tax adviser.

If your world includes a small business or other activities that go beyond a simple tax return, professional advice can save you many painful experiences. Even those who have a very basic tax return can benefit from tax planning.

It is not only avoiding the negative experience of making a mistake on your income tax return that leads to an assessment or penalty. Engaging someone to advise you on this area of the financial world ensures that you are receiving all of the deductions and credits to which you are entitled.

Perhaps most importantly, using an accountant or tax adviser helps you plan successfully. As we discussed elsewhere in the book, you want to have the answer to the "What is left in my pocket?" question that always includes not only your investment choice and inflation, but taxes, as well. They need to be involved in advance of your decisions to help you make choices that fit your objectives – after taxes.

As with your other professionals, choose the best adviser you can afford at the time. They are an investment. You may already know someone you trust, or you might want to check out those recommended to you by people you trust.

*Trust* is an important word when it comes to any of your advisers. You want to find someone who will truly listen to you rather than hand you a cookie-cutter solution. The expert should be that. That does not exclude younger advisers. Some of them through education and perspective have a great sense of what is going on that is sometimes sharper than one on the other end of the continuum who is just coasting to the finish line. What is key is that you can be honest with them.

Being honest includes sharing your dreams. These might be totally unrealistic for where you are today. Dreams do happen with the right ingredients. Share your fears, too. Let that adviser know what worries you and what concerns you have as you look down the road. Expect to hear alternatives from a good adviser that gives you the choice of different paths. Each path often requires different levels of commitment and sacrifice from you to achieve the goals. Understanding these choices helps you make informed decisions.

The bottom line with an adviser is just that – they are there to advise, not decide. Many people look at the world of finance and declare that it is too complicated to understand. Tax law certainly is complex.

The best an adviser can do for you is to clearly explain the choices or options you should consider. Hopefully, he will explain the pros and cons of each of those roads. But at the end of the day, it is your decision.

Many people complain about how their world turned out because they received bad advice. In some cases, that may be true. More often, people are disappointed by the bad choices they made. Hold yourself accountable for the financial decisions you make. You may have ups and downs, as well as unexpected events that shatter your plans. If that happens, it is okay to be disappointed, but own the choices you made along the journey. It makes the possibility of recovery that much more likely because you are not shifting responsibility elsewhere.

So when it comes to tax planning, do not wait until April to find out what your refund will be. Start planning in May to make the next year and the years ahead ones that include a great tax strategy.

# CLIMATE VS. WEATHER

Some people are local experts when it comes to changes in the weather. Whether it is through the use of advanced technology, constantly checking forecasts or just a feeling in their bones, they always seem to know what is going to happen. It is going to rain today. Colder weather is coming tomorrow.

Then there are the people who care more about what is happening around the world. A typhoon in Asia, extreme drought in the southwest and flooding in the northeast can be in any news cycle, it seems. They are fascinated by the changes in the jet streams and the tropical depressions forming off the west coast of Africa. These people like the big picture.

When it comes to the financial winds that blow in our world, we need to know about both the weather and the climate. As you may recall from your earlier science classes, the weather describes the changing local conditions, whereas the climate describes the larger, long-term trends in the general region where you live. Therefore, in the financial and investment world, it is wise to pay attention to what is happening locally and to the larger financial climate. We may be affected by our local conditions, or our local conditions might be changed by what is happening a world away.

Globalization makes this everyone's business.

A positive economic climate usually exists where the right mix of demand for goods and services is combined with governments that have created conditions in which business can grow and thrive. In an ideal world, that means lower and more predictable taxes, moderate inflation, steady interest rates, stable energy prices, low unemployment and a stable social system. Of course, we rarely get to see that ideal picture. Depending on what part or parts of the picture have been clouded, different parts of the economy – and ultimately our personal world – will be at risk.

A period when things are going well is called a *recovery* – even if the recovery grows higher than it was before it fell. Down periods are called *recessions* if the main measures of the economy have two negative quarters in a row. That means that the economy is dropping for at least six months in a row in order to qualify as a recession. So you will hear commentators talk about the economy "expanding" or "contracting."

Paying attention to commentaries on what the business and investment climate is can be very helpful. Sometimes the commentaries will disagree – especially if politics are involved. But as you watch the trend lines, you will usually see whether we are heading toward better times or worse ones.

When you see trends turning negative, that is a time to get ahead of the crowd and reduce your risks. Those risks can be increasing your cash reserves, reducing your debt and perhaps being more conservative in your shorter-term investments.

After a negative period, you can begin to see improvement in the leading indicators that suggest better times have begun. Those are times when it is wise to consider making more investments and increasing your level of risk.

There are some periods of time when the indicators seem to be holding in place for a while. The stock market is said to be going sideways. It is not clear when the breakthrough will begin.

For the average person, you do not want to be the first out of a recession or the first into one. There is usually a great deal of volatility as the marketplace is changing. Back to our weather analogy, a new front coming through often brings storms as the weather settles in for a change.

So pay attention to what is happening locally, as it can impact your employer and community. But do not miss the larger climate that exists that will make it easier or more difficult for employers to expand their businesses.

# IT'S A SMALL WORLD AFTER ALL

Globalization is, for some people, a sign of great progress. For others it is a word that has doomed industries that have been at the core of our economy for years. There are many issues that could be debated on that topic – for and against.

For our purposes in this book, let us deal with the fact that it is here. Communication, transportation, and information all travel at speeds that have made our very wide world shrink in just a generation.

This is not a new phenomenon. The effect of every empire (once it was established) was to create the infrastructure (such as roads and shipping) along with the government and often language that opened the world to a new level of trade. This happened in ancient times in the Middle East and in Asia. It was one of the facts of the Roman Empire that is still astonishing today. The lack of empire shows itself after Rome fell when the European countries fell into the Dark Ages for centuries. Later empires from Europe once again reinvigorated trade, knowledge and opportunity. The British Empire made the wide world smaller through its navy and extensive trading companies. The American domination post-Cold War created the conditions to expand trade in all directions.

Cheap oil allowed goods to move around the world so that automobile manufacturing could migrate from Detroit to Japan and South Korea. Textiles could move from the Southern U.S. to China and Malaysia.

The BRIC countries (Brazil, Russia, India and China) are new forces competing with Europe and the United States, which have been distracted by war and a false sense of economic security. Brazil and Russia have energy resources as a big part of their strength. India and China have their huge, emerging populations that can have economies of scale that get things done cheaply compared to the more mature economies with their aging populations.

Why bring this up in a book on personal finance and investment? These big trends will have an impact on you and your family's future. Just as with other areas of your personal plan, you must take personal responsibility to make yourself competitive.

Does all of this spell gloom and doom for people in the United States, Canada, Australia or Europe? Not at all! Every country has some special advantages built into it. Whether and how they will use these advantages will make the difference in the future that our children and we will experience.

Globalization means that production, information and increasingly services can be accessed anywhere in the world. That means that the local economy has to be ready to compete with other places around the world that are trying to attract economic activity. If you are doing what everyone else does – watch out. If you are doing what everyone else does and you cost much more than your competitors – you are in real danger. Investment follows opportunity. Higher costs and higher wages often are seen as stop signs by people who might otherwise invest in your area.

What can you do about it?

Look for ways to provide extra value in what you do. One of the most important elements of being competitive (and therefore an attractive place to invest) is attitude. In the workplace, that means an attitude of real customer service. No matter what our role in the company, government or service we provide, our commitment must be to excellence. We cannot risk doing any less than our very best. Poor customer service and poor quality labour soon eliminate any savings of working in a developing country. Excellent attitudes will create excellent opportunities.

The other helpful piece of the puzzle is to have strong communities. Businesses thrive in stable and positive places. Communities that invest in their well-being through sharing time and treasure create an advantage that companies will factor into their decision. After all, company managers and employees have to live in the communities where their businesses exist. Making your community a place that they would want to live can increase productivity and make your area a better investment.

On a personal level, you will make yourself a more essential part of any organization if you have the disciplines of excellence in your attitude toward your career and those you serve through it.

It may be a small world, but you can still carve out your own piece of it to grow.

# COPING WITH A CRISIS

It is a fact of life that everyone will face a crisis – maybe more than one over the course of their lifetime. By a crisis, I mean when something happens that brings you to a point of major decision. Sometimes a crisis happens suddenly like a car accident or an illness. Other points of crisis could be seen coming for a long time. Whether they are ignored with the hope that they would go away or brought on by choices that did not prevent them – either way, it's trouble.

One of the advantages of time and perspective is that if you have experienced a crisis before, you are better able to handle the next one. (Note to self – do not look for a crisis to become expert in them – they will find you soon enough!) When you have been able to survive a crisis, you learn what helps and what does not in dealing with a problem that is now urgent. Like so many things in life, it is the preparations we make ahead of the crisis that give us the tools and temperament to survive a major challenge when it hits. Every time you face a problem and solve it, you add tools to your emotional and mental toolbox that can be used in the next crisis.

One of the most important lessons that you learn in enduring a crisis is the fact that there is the other side of the event. Whatever image you want to use, whether it is climbing the mountain, going through the valley or crossing the deep river, understand that many others have faced and survived a challenge similar to yours. Some of the details of the crisis will be different, and each one is unique in some way. However, the problems faced in our human experience are largely the same.

Here are some steps you can take when you face a crisis.

Begin by saying that you will get through it. You need to have the optimism and courage to face whatever the "it" is in your crisis effectively. That does not minimize how difficult or tough it may be. You may face pain, loss or the unknown. But your attitude going into the crisis is a big factor in how you will come through the challenges.

Work to define as quickly as you can what the "it" in the crisis is. You might think that this is obvious, but sometimes there are layers to get through to get down to the challenge level. If you have a car accident, is the "it" for you an injury or the cost of fixing/replacing your car, or the need for temporary transportation or just the shock that it happened? Depending on your circumstances, you may have a very different point of crisis from someone else who also had a car accident. Try to get to the core of the crisis.

Next, identify who can help. Perhaps it is your financial adviser if you have a financial crisis. If it is a health crisis, your doctor or other health professional is key. If the crisis is in a relationship, perhaps speaking with a trusted counsellor or minister can help. Usually there is room for family members or friends to be there to give us encouragement, perspective and support in a crisis too. Ask others who may have faced a similar crisis what helped them through the experience.

Finally, look at the benefits of facing the crisis. Often, a crisis will trigger change. Change can be scary for many people. The loss of a job is a crisis. But it can also lead us to a different set of opportunities if we have been preparing for the unemployment risk that all of us face. Once you have identified the alternatives, work out the step-by-step plan to work through the challenges. As you go through the hard times, understand that this will become part of your story. None of us would choose the difficult chapters in our life's story, but all of our stories are much more interesting because of what we have survived.

# OIL CHANGES

In an age in which an economy breathes or chokes on the price of oil, understanding what is happening in the energy industry can make the difference between growth or recession.

We tend to think of it when we visit the gas station and fill up our car – or only do a partial fill-up because of the price! Every time when spend money on energy, those are dollars that are not available to spend or invest elsewhere. So much of life includes an energy cost that you can see why keeping an eye on the price of energy is important financially.

Beyond the gas pump, energy prices factor into our cost of living in obvious and subtle ways. The electricity bill is easy to connect. The price of the fruit and vegetables that were transported to you are also affected by the cost of energy. Manufacturing that uses a great deal of energy to produce their product will have to pass on the higher energy costs to you when you purchase their item or risk cutting their profit margin.

Everywhere that there are goods and services that are directly affected by the price of crude oil and natural gas, the economy will feel the effects. If you take enough money out of other purchases because of the higher costs of energy, companies make less money and begin the process of slowing hiring and spending. Before you know it, the companies stop hiring and then start to lay off workers. Communities that were functioning well with the incomes of their employees of their city or town suddenly face the prospect of less activity for all of them. If this happens for a long enough time, the shock becomes the new normal, and that is how a recession can begin.

Some economists have suggested that the housing crisis and the economic collapse of the Bush-Obama years in the United States were not a result of the housing bubble being burst by the risky loan schemes. Rather, it was the spike in energy costs that took money away from corporations that led them to cut back on jobs and investment. Before long, individuals and families no longer had the income needed to pay for their increasing mortgage costs along with everything else. Once the mortgages went unpaid and then went into default, housing values went down as more and more homes were put on the market for sale. That created the downward spiral that collapsed the housing market in so many areas of the U.S.

The housing market was vulnerable because of the bubble and the ownership by people who could not afford the increasing cost of the mortgages they signed. However, energy may have been the pin that burst the bubble.

So pay attention to changes in the price of energy. When it is rising due to increased demand or uncertainties around the world, be sure to raise your financial caution flag, too. When energy prices are comparatively low, take that as an opportunity to reduce your debt and give yourself added flexibility for the next time the cost of energy goes up again.

# TICK-TOCK

Time is both our friend and our enemy. When we are younger, it is our friend. But being newer to life, we tend not to recognize that it is something that will journey with us all day, every day until we die.

Buying a house, marriage, children, career changes, midlife crisis, mortgage burning, children's education, retirement, late retirement healthcare and finally death are all just distant concepts to someone who is just finishing school. Some of these life passages may be in focus, but many are not. Those are for tomorrow's worries and plans. We do know in concept that we only have today and that life could end in an instant. However, when you are young and vigorous, death is a subject best left to those on the high side of eighty years old to consider.

In the rapidly accelerating set of experiences that accompany becoming an adult, our young friend time soon becomes a competitor in middle age. We race against time to achieve our dreams as soon as possible. Then, like a winded runner at the end of a marathon, we look up and see that time looks just as fresh as ever and ready to lap us. As we grow older, time seems to pass us by more quickly each year. Eventually we get used to this and wave as time makes it around the track once more.

If we are wise, we will learn to make friends with time when we are young. That means that we will begin planning our financial future when we are young enough to let our money grow "over time." We want time to take what we set aside for our future and allow it to grow year after year. In this way, we are hiring our money to work for us over time so that we can reach the point where it is doing the work – not us. The earlier you begin and the more you contribute to your medium and retirement investments, the sooner you will be earning enough from your investments to give you many more choices down the road.

So, if you are young or know someone who is, make friends with time so that it can be your lifelong friend. At any point along the journey, you can befriend time. So, if you are now in your thirties, forties or even fifties – time can still be a friend. If you are older than your fifties, it still is important to make the best decisions with what you do have, since depending on your longevity, you may be living and spending for another thirty or forty years.

Pay attention to that tick-tock that you hear off in the distance. It will not be long before it sounds like you are standing under Big Ben and you will not only hear but also feel every one of those gongs that remind you that time is passing.

# THE SAGE

Down through the ages, great kings have always had a sage to guide them. Usually these were older persons who served as a private counsellor to the king or queen. Trusted and loyal, the monarch could count on them to give their best advice. We are familiar with them from Biblical times as prophets like Samuel or Nathan who advised and guided the early kings of Israel. In some tales, a magician like Merlin was there for King Arthur. In Middle Earth, it was Gandalf for Aragorn, Théoden and other great leaders. Today it can be a chief of staff to a president or an elder statesman to the prime minister. Even former presidents and prime ministers are consulted for their perspectives by their successors.

These advisers provide wisdom and perspective that come from their experience. They also can give a balancing view to help the person in the center of the storm step back to understand what she or he is facing. A truly great sage can confront their leader and tell the person when he or she is off track. The monarch may not like to hear it, but it is a huge advantage to have someone who will "speak the truth" to you. People who will say what they think the leader wants to hear, (out of respect or fear or sometimes manipulation) surround so many leaders. Leaders need to have someone they can trust to tell them how they are doing.

For those of us who are in a committed relationship, hopefully we have the benefit of that spouse who will encourage us as well as help us step on the brake from time to time. In life, we also need to have someone else who is outside of the marriage relationship that can be that trusted sage for us as a couple, as well. If you are privileged to have someone who can serve as a mentor for you, you are blessed. If you do not have someone in that role, look around and seek that kind of person out of your network of family and friends.

The sage still leaves the decision and the responsibility up to you. We cannot duck the challenges of our life by blaming someone else for the choices we make. But we will make better choices if we have established that kind of trusting relationship with someone who has been on the road longer than ourselves to guide and coach us through the ups and downs of life.

Many computer games hearken back to an age that includes the challenges of facing dragons, trolls and other unsavory creatures. Before leaving home, most of these games have you form a party of friends to face the uncertain road ahead. In addition to the warriors, it is usually a good idea to take a wizard with you.

No matter what your age or stage, it is good to have some old friends who will be there for you to walk down the dark roads at your side. Bring a sage along if you want to make it back with your treasure intact.

# LEARNING TO BE WEALTHY

Education is a topic that is discussed everywhere. It is a very important part of your financial future, too. Decisions you make in high school affect your possibilities for university or college in the future. Choices you make in college and university will greatly affect your potential for a career that you enjoy. It also will influence how much money you earn over your working career, which will in turn change the possibilities you have down the road.

This is not to say that you cannot add to your education when you are older. It is never too late to continue your education. But our system is set up to give you the most opportunities and the easiest path to success if you can complete your secondary school and university or college experience along with the others your age. In our competitive society and global economy, the better educated have some very real advantages in getting and keeping the best jobs. We will not try to cover all of the territory on this subject, as there are many good books and resources there to help you. However, we will try to connect the dots between your education and your long-term financial health.

The first thing to understand is that the best education is not one that "gets you a job." Vocational education is useful. Professional schools in engineering, medicine and law are all valuable. However, many people who focus on the equation that a good education equals a specific job ignore some of the realities of our world today. They also shortchange themselves on some of what is best in learning. So, here are some radical ideas for you to consider.

**A great education is to teach you how to learn.**

You probably have heard the phrase "lifelong learning" in recent years. This is a statement about how rapidly the workplace is changing and how we need to be able to upgrade our knowledge and skills throughout our working life. People with a great education have an advantage; because they have learned *how* to learn, *what* they need to learn is less important because they already know *how* to learn along the way as needed. We all learn differently. Some are visual learners. Others learn better by hearing ideas expressed. Some learn best by doing or what is called "kinetic" learning. Many are a combination.

School – especially traditional education taught by teachers who have lost their motivation to enchant their classes – can be a difficult place for many people to endure. "What's the point of this?" Like many areas of life, it is up to us to "own" our education. No one will care about our education or career as much as we do. If you are not getting the most from your courses or teachers, take responsibility to change that by changing schools, course or teachers. Another approach is to supplement your learning from the many wonderful resources on many subjects available online, on DVDs and in books. Do not settle for a bad education. Do not let a tired educational system or boring teachers chase you away from what you need and deserve for a great future.

As our world is changing rapidly, the kinds of jobs that are available (and where they are available) seems to change at the speed of light. It was not so many years ago that if you listened to the "experts," we should all be training to operate keypunch machines (for old computer data entry cards) and be able to speak Russian (in case the Soviet Union took over someday.) People who target their education toward a job often end up preparing for the work of the last generation, which has disappeared by the time they enter the workforce.

However, if you have concentrated on learning how to learn, you carry that most important skill set with you. Once you begin a job, you find out that many of the details of your education are not relevant as you learn the specific requirements of a job, no matter how well trained you are at school.

The next big idea is that a great education is to teach you about life. It improves you as a person because you learn to think about areas that are new to you. If you are a good student, a broad education in which you sample from many of the disciplines of study is a huge advantage throughout your life. The best problem solvers, inventors and creative people connect ideas from different places to come up with a new solution. A broad education also teaches you about yourself and others. Self-awareness and social skills always make you a more valuable employee or leader. Unless you are one of those people with a very specific passion or gift that brings you to a focus in your education early, stay broad like a classic liberal arts education until you get to the master's degree level where you can specialize.

If you are going to a vocational college for a specific career, do not despise the general courses you might have to take. These can help you be a cut above the others who will be competing for that job you want in the future.

Stay in school as long as you can in your younger years. Those years of education are just like a savings plan because they will follow you throughout your life to give you some advantages over those who took the quick route out of school.

Keep adding to your education to continue your personal and professional development. These investments of time and treasure will pay off over a lifetime.

# IN GOOD COMPANY

Your career begins long before your first job and continues long after you retire. Like pages in your book of life, they are written before we know much about the characters and continue until their story is over with all of the twists and turns along the way.

As you begin your working life, you will be in the lifelong adventure of discovering and defining your career. The jobs you take or choose not to take each move you down the career path that often is not really understood until you look backwards.

To be sure, most people have short or long periods of time in which they take and keep a job because that is all they can get at the time to pay the bills. Our careers take off is in those moments when the opportunities to work connect with our passions. We get to do the work we love to do. As the old adage says, "If you love what you do, you will never have to work a day in your life."

So whenever possible, keep the promise to yourself to find and grow the jobs that use your talents and passions to make a difference in not just your bank account, but your world, as well.

Recognize that any company, no matter how great it is as an employer, is renting your time and talent. Make sure that they and you are getting the most out of that arrangement by giving them your best. If you have an attitude that is committed to making those around you in the company a success, you will find that you, too, will be successful – and often indispensable. People who concentrate on themselves tend to have less impact through their job and a career of "might have beens" that are lost to a selfish view of what it means to be doing a solid day's work and going the extra mile.

If you have never examined what it is that motivates you to give your best, spend some time exploring that topic. Take the tests that help you to find what kinds of jobs fit with your talents and passions. All of those efforts will reward you and your career with a life worth living.

Once you have figured those things out, then you can start making choices with your jobs that are not just about what combination of pay and benefits are being offered.

That will help you not only to own your career, but your future, as well.

# THE ENTREPRENEUR - THE GOOD, THE BAD AND THE UGLY

Which side of the check do you want to sign? If you are the kind of person who wants the security of someone else signing your cheque, then being an employee is a great thing. You can rent your time to those who are your employers and they will pay you for that time in the form of a paycheck and perhaps benefits and a pension as well. If you are an employee, you make this exchange each workday. Employees sign the back of their cheque when they deposit it.

If you want to sign the front of the check then you have taken the first step toward being the boss. If you are an employer or are self-employed, you sign the front of the cheque. Which side of the check you sign makes a huge difference in so many aspects of your life – now and in the future. Is one better than the other? That depends on who you are and what you are willing to do.

Many people spend much of their working life dreaming of the opportunity to be in charge of their day and to be in business on their own. But the life of an entrepreneur is not as easy as it sounds. After reading this chapter, you may have a new respect for those many people who are crazy enough to create and operate a business. Get them during a quiet moment (if you can find one with them) and they will tell you about the challenges of the independent businessperson's life.

Being your own boss is an especially popular topic in a difficult economy. Many find it challenging or impossible to convince someone to hire them. Many older employees will never return to the kind of jobs that were part of their employment story when manufacturing was more plentiful and wages were high. If you have come to a crossroad, you may need to consider the alternatives. Further training and education is an option. Improving your ability to sell yourself is another. Maybe you need to be your own boss and you no longer have a choice about it. Before you give up on working again, one of the choices to consider is to hire yourself.

If so, there are things that you can do to make that an easier transition and to make your adventure successful. (It is never a venture – it is always an adventure!)

If you are one of those people who have skills or passion or an interest in providing a product or service, then being in business may be something you should consider. As much as we have gone through many negative or challenging parts of what it means to be on your own, it is a certainly very rewarding type of career when you come home each day, knowing that you made a difference in the customers that you served.

The first that thing to point out is that many in businesses do not just start with the idea of selling a product. That is something that would have been more typical in past decades. Now it is more likely that you would be selling a service rather than a product. Selling a service reflects the idea that you have some skill or some ability that other people or other companies would want to employ. While that service can be offered through an employer, there are many services that employers are willing to outsource or buy on a contract basis, as they need them. As companies downsize, one of the things they look at is hiring people for a specific project or a specific task rather than having them inside the company. This is a growing area of the labor market.

What does it take to be an entrepreneur?

It is something that involves many different aspects of motivation, skills, confidence, and the ability to visualize. You do not have to be good at everything to be an entrepreneur, but you must have a solution for each aspect of what it means to run a small business. You do not have to be an accountant, but you need to know someone who can do your books or help you with your tax returns. You do not have to be someone who knows all of the answers in terms of the technical aspects of your business, but you need to know where you would go, who you would call, or who you would e-mail for those things that you do not know in the service that you are providing. If you are distributing a product, you have to understand how long it takes to get the product to you, what the cost of purchasing those products is, and how you would inventory the level of products that you would want to have on hand to resell to people through your business.

Each business has its own cycle; there are businesses that are more typical in terms of the time of year. If you are selling services related to holidays, obviously you get for the holidays. You have a very intense period, and then you have a less activity as you go past those holidays and start planning for the following year. Other businesses are seasonal because they provide services that are weather-related or year-related. If you look at air-conditioning, obviously that is something that is more important during the hot weather if you are in an environment where there is a seasonal change. Similarly, if you are someone who is providing a tax preparation service, this will be something that would be busier and more involved as you ran up to the year end and as you get to the tax-filing season.

You will need an understanding of what kinds of cycles that there would be for your year, whether it is something that I would have consistent sales or whether it is something that would have some intense times of activity and then other times when it would not be quite so intense.

It is a good thing to get some advice on starting a small business. Everyone's situation is different. Programs are available both from nonprofit agencies as well as from government services designed to help you succeed in a small business. There are also programs through a local Chamber of Commerce and other entrepreneurial organizations that will be there as a resource to help you understand what it means to start a business. They will look with you at what choices you can make so your business opportunity will have the best prospect of success.

Some things that are true no matter what kind of business you consider starting. Here are some of the ingredients that need to be there for all businesses. Check out the particulars of your business products or services to see how these ideas apply to your situation.

The first thing would be to recognize that being in your own business means that you are going to work harder than you ever have in your life. If you have the illusion that "being your own boss" means that you have less work to do and that your life would be suddenly and instantly carefree, you are on the wrong track. For most people, starting a business requires a tremendous amount of energy and motivation just to get things organized before you get rolling. Once you are in the business and it is actually working for you, you still have to think of it as hiring yourself each day and asking the next day, "Did I work hard enough that I would hire myself again?" If the answer to that is no, then you really have to level up the work that needs to be done. The business of an entrepreneur is only going to be as effective and successful as the person's motivation and commitment to do the hard work required. Most people in small businesses work more hours per day, per week, and per year than other people who are employed by someone else.

All of this is very challenging and might cause you to wonder why bother?

The answer is that there are rewards in being an entrepreneur. Those who start their own business can have the possibility of creating something that becomes an asset and that is different from those who are renting their time as an employee. It also gives you some flexibility and freedom to develop yourself and to focus your energies and your motivation. Most people can only earn so many dollars per day or per year based on whatever the agreed wages as an hourly wage or salary. Working for yourself, you have the upside of being able to make more. It is not a fixed destiny.

However, the downside is also true. The consistency of a paycheck is something that is very valuable. For people who are not really certain of what they want to do, having the security of a regular paycheck is something that must not be discounted. However, if you are in a situation where you just cannot take it anymore and you are willing to take the risk, you may be willing to make the great leap. There are no guarantees for people who are on their own. You can put in a hard day's work, and depending on what product your service you are selling, you may get many sales, some or none.

You have the uncertainty but also the possibility that comes with being on your own. That uncertainty can be something that is very exciting and motivational or it could cause you great dread and fear. Understanding your personality type, your experience, and your own sense of confidence is an important element in deciding whether or not you should go into business on your own.

Beyond that, another consideration is your financial resources; it takes money to start a business. Even if you are starting one that seems simple, not requiring many products as inventory, there are many costs associated with just getting started. As you are not making money from an employer, you need money set aside for you to be able to live on and to pay your bills that are there day in and day out until your business can support you.

Secondly, you also need to be able to start up whatever marketing supplies that you need. That can be as simple as a business card, a website that you need or some other tools to get your name out there. You may need money to get those things in place prior to actually receiving any money from a sale or from a service call that you make. You have to think this through very carefully and have the necessary resources. Whatever you think your budget is, you need to make it larger. Whatever you think your expenses are going to be, people spend more than they expect. Sales usually take longer to turn into cash in the bank that you could imagine. It is a real advantage if you can have money set aside that is more than you need to get through a number of months of start-up with the understanding that you may take a long time to actually develop your customers and have that kind of regular income that would support you in the longer term. How long that will be depends on you as an individual and the kind of business you are looking at. It is useful to talk to other people who are in start-up situations or those from government or other services that help entrepreneurs' small businesses get going.

Another aspect of this is having a good relationship with your bank, trust company, or other financial institution. You cannot suddenly just venture out on your own and stop the regular paycheck that they thought would always be there for you. That can adversely affect such things as your credit and your ability to keep a mortgage. You really need to understand this thoroughly before you venture out. You want to talk to your advisors about how to deal with your bank or the financial institution as you are considering making a big move like that. Many people work well when they have one partner in the family who is receiving the regular income and the other person is part of starting the business. When you are in that situation, you can have the best of both worlds. The upside of the entrepreneur and the consistent income from traditional employment is that it helps to pay those regular bills that come in whether you are having a great sales week or not.

Another way to approach this is to start your business on the side while you continue your present job. If you are in a company or situation where you are allowed to do that, it is wise to check and make sure that there are no conflicts of interest or other requirements in your contract that preclude you from doing that. It may be a good thing to try and start your business or service on the side in a small way. That will give you a chance to test the waters and to learn some of the early lessons you need to learn about your business while still giving you the opportunity to get going.

Another element that is very crucial to your business venture is to have a good sense of who you are. For anyone in any kind of business, you need to be able to sell yourself and to demonstrate to people why they want to do business with you. It is not enough to say that you have a great product, because they are not just buying the product; they are buying a relationship with you. They may be able to get the product somewhere else, so if you are not being effective in your relationship with them, you will not be able to have a successful business. You really have to understand how to sell yourself as part of the transaction, and that is especially true if you are providing a service, whether it is consulting or some other service that you are providing. People will often give you a first chance to see how it works out, but they are not likely to come back if you are not giving them excellent customer service and a show a commitment to them. That involves selling yourself in a way that is effective, giving clients confidence you know what you are doing. They need to know you are committed to serving them.

The world of the new business really survives on that. It grows through word-of-mouth from satisfied customers or satisfied businesses who tell others that you are someone worth hiring. They know they will receive good customer service, good value and a great attitude.

On the flip side, if you are in a situation in which you provide less than your best, then the companies will say, "Thank you very much," and will pay the bill but they will not hire you again. You want each of the experiences that they have to be top-notch and to be something where you sold yourself well. You need to be somebody who cares about giving them the very best and actually delivering on that. Referrals are a huge part of how small businesses grow, so you want to be in a situation in which you can feel comfortable asking for those referrals. If you ask someone at the end of the sale for an evaluation, it gives an opportunity to think about giving you a referral. As you get a good response to someone saying, "We are happy with the work you've done," you can ask directly or indirectly (depending on your approach and what you are providing) to say, "Is there is anybody else that you can think of who could benefit from this? I appreciate your recommendation." Alternatively, you might ask them for a reference by saying, "Could I bother you for a paragraph or two just describing how we did for you, so that I can use that to let other people know about the products or services that we provide?" Those are good tools for that.

Another thing to consider is the importance of selling intangibles. Intangibles are things you cannot touch or hold. We may tend to think of that as being a service or a certain kind of product like insurance or investments. However, everyone needs to understand how to sell intangibles because every product— a car, washing machine, vitamins, or anything else—has some intangible qualities to it. Every sale therefore has an intangible aspect to it. You have to be able to understand what is going on in the sales process and be able to sell the story and the idea along with the product or service. The reason that some people will get hired and others will not has more to do with how they were able to position the story of their product or service is the one to buy or hire versus the competition.

We are back to that big question.

Do you want to be your own boss?

This comes back to the idea of being a boss. The reality is that none of us is the boss. Even if you think that you are working for yourself, you really are working for someone else. That might not be an employer in a traditional sense, but you are working for your customers. If you have the attitude of serving customers to make them successful with whatever service or product that you provide, then you too will be successful. We are always in the business of serving customers, whether we are in government, industry, or education—anything that we are doing is really serving other people. The better we serve them, the more effective we will be in our careers, and the better we will be able to look back on our story and enjoy the fact that we made a difference in the life that we lived.

In interviews with seniors where they reflect on their life, one of the common themes that is heard is that they wished they had taken more risks when they were younger. They also often wish that they had spent more time doing what they loved.

What should you do? Consider the possibilities. Do not make your decision out of fear. Whatever you decide, plan it well, get advice, assess the risks and discover whether you it is for you. Then give yourself to it so that whatever you do as an employee or as an entrepreneur you are the best at serving others and making a difference. That will be a story worth telling in the sunset years of your life.

# A CREATIVE TOUCH

One of the most desirable qualities in the competitive workplace is having a creative touch. It is that extra creative flair that can separate you from the many others who have similar resumes and work histories. The edge that a creative approach gives to an employer is not what you might think.

Creativity is a sign of flexibility.

People who are willing to be creative are obviously open to doing something in a new or different way. That is the root of the word – to create. To *create* is the opposite of to *repeat*.

We live in a world where repeating the same old processes or answers to our challenges is no longer good enough. It is not enough to keep the status quo. Individuals who have made careers out of keeping your head down and trying to avoid being noticed now find themselves looking for work. That is because companies can no longer afford to settle for what worked ten or twenty years ago. The forces of global competition, technology and innovation have touched virtually all careers.

If you are physician, it is not enough to live off of what you learned in med school.

If you are in government, it is not enough to say that this is what we have always done.

If you are a teacher, it is not enough to regurgitate the curriculum.

If you are in business, it is not enough to operate the same way you did twenty years ago.

If you are an entrepreneur, you already get that.

If you are inventor, you live that.

So how do you add creativity to your portfolio of talents and abilities? It is true that some people are naturally creative – especially in areas in which we think of creative expression.  Some people are artists, musicians, dancers, authors, actors and poets. We think of these people of being inspired, talented and gifted. The good ones are. The great ones certainly are.

Perhaps you feel like you are someone on the other end of the spectrum. You are the reliable type of person who can follow instructions and carry out tasks reliably.  Maybe you are one of those highly disciplined people who can follow details with no problem.  But you might wonder how it is that you could be creative.

For perspective, understand that people who seem to be naturally creative are not always disciplined.  For many of them, the very gifts that bombard them with everything new and different make it tough for them to get it done. Getting it done takes discipline. Most of the starving artists never produced enough paintings, had the discipline to market them successfully or perhaps were not artists at all.  It is a challenge for most creative people to add the discipline required to actually create and then do the follow-up editing or tasks required for their work to be truly accessible.

The flip side is true for the people who are not naturally creative. You must learn to add creativity to your discipline. How do you do that? It is not easy, but you can do it.

Creativity begins with a question. It might be "Why not?" Sometimes it is "What else?" "Is there a better way?" or "What if?" These and many other questions are asked routinely by creative people.

Questions are normal for the disciplined person, as well. They routinely ask, "What is expected?" or "How do I get this finished?"

Adding that new set of questions will begin the creative process for those who do not feel naturally creative. Just giving yourself permission to ask those "What if?" questions will create opportunities for change and a fresh look.

The other tool to enhance your creativity is knowledge. Creative people often know many things about a wide range of subjects. A liberal arts education is one of the best preparations to have that broad and creative approach, since you learn a little bit about the wide range subject areas that are covered. Expanding your knowledge will give you more potential connections.

The process of invention is to take things that are not currently connected and put them together in a new and different way. Often that includes a great deal of experimentation and failure. However, the creative process is driven by this new way of sorting the information or solving a problem. The broader your experiences and knowledge, the more connections you can create. Included in that is participating in creative experiences. That could be watching a play or listening to a concert. It can even be walking in a beautiful garden where you can notice that variety and arrangement of flowers and other plants. Stimulating your senses invites creativity. Even better would be finding ways to participate in creative activities yourself. You may have had experiences when you were younger with a musical instrument or some form of art or drama. Dust off that old flute or take an art class. Join a choir. Get involved. All of these things help.

Then when it comes to your work, add the creative touch. Look for new and better ways to do your job, teach your class, or serve your customers. Build creativity into your day, just like the creative types need to add discipline to be successful.

Lastly, be sure to add it to your resume and make it part of your personal presentation at any interview. That creative flair may get you that next job or promotion.

# GROWING UP

The healthy and appropriate track for each of us as we are growing up is to go through the developmental stages of dependence, independence, and finally, as mature people, we become interdependent. This is the path for all healthy individuals to reach their potential as people and in society.

Each of the stages is unique. We begin with dependence without a choice or a possibility of anything different. It is impossible for newborn human beings to survive on their own. They are dependent. Each one needs the basic necessities of food, clothing and shelter. They also need nurturing. Children thrive when they have loving, attentive adults who hold them, talk to them and assure them that they are loved. Trust is developed as children experience the wider world. Children learn from the spoken and unspoken cues from the others in their world. Their world expands from the immediate family to the larger world of their community and beyond. Their education that begins from their first breath becomes more formalized as they enter school and continue a lifetime of learning.

Children ease from the stage of being totally dependent to the beginnings of independence. Learning to choose what object they grab, what toy to play with and what food to eat first are all hints of their growing sense of self. Learning to walk and the other early life passages continue them along this journey. They start to see themselves as not just a member of the family but as a unique member different from the others. Their unique personality traits start to express that they are special. Later, being at school encourages them to begin to not just depend on others but to start to do things on their own. They become accountable for their behaviour in their play and work. Slowly but surely they start to rely on themselves as they sort out who they are. This continues subtly until the teenage years, when most children go through a period in which they assert their independence to a greater or lesser degree depending on the child and their family system. The many confrontations and powerful changes in hormones reflect the growing independence as the child becomes a man or a woman. There is a separation that distinguishes them from their parents, family and the child they once were. This is a wrenching experience for all involved, but it is a necessary one for individuals to become adults. Without this important passage, they will always be dependent.

It is tragic to see someone who never learned to become independent as a person. It is just as tragic for people who were stuck at the independent stage and never fully matured to the next part of the journey. Fully functioning and well-adjusted adults have reached the stage of interdependence. This too is a subtle process in which an independent individual recognizes that he, too, benefits from his other relationships. But unlike the first stage in which she or he is dependent, he or she enters these relationships as one who is both giving and receiving from others. Each one contributes who and what she or he is to the family or social group. That makes the group stronger, and therefore it strengthens all of the individuals who are part of the group, as well.

The interdependent adult invests his time and energy in the development of the others in society. Families and societies that provide for their dependent children, suffer the traumas of allowing them to become independent, and then encourage interdependence are the communities in which everyone can thrive.

That is a future worth owning.

# FAMILY STYLE

It is said that "God chose your family so you could choose your friends!" While there is truth in that statement, it is also true that "blood is thicker than water."

Families can be an important source of security on many levels. It begins with our most basic needs of food, shelter and safety. It also hopefully begins with the emotional security that comes from being loved and nurtured from our earliest moments. As we develop, we learn to trust and depend on others for our well-being. Eventually, we begin to make our contribution to the health of the family unit through our participation, caring and support in return. In a healthy family, these bonds are created and strengthened over one's lifetime.

That is not to say that family members are the same. Some are very similar in temperament and interests. Others are so different that it seems a study should be commissioned to see how two siblings can come from the same parentage and experiences growing up and yet be so different. That is the wonder of families.

It is often true that different family members have different experiences and insights that can benefit the rest of the family. This applies not just to the nuclear family of parents and children but to aunts, uncles, grandparents and cousins, too. If you are blessed with a larger family group, invest time and care into the larger circle. Eventually you will find times when you will need their insight or counsel when you run into a challenge.

Strong families are an important building block financially as well as socially and spiritually. Many studies show that a strong family unit is a positive force that gives individuals a much better future on many levels of life. The presence of two parents in the home is perhaps one of the most essential elements for predicting the future success of the children. Single-parent families require great courage and sacrifice by the parent who is present. Their efforts are to be valued and recognized, but it is no substitute for a two-parent family when it comes to the needs of children. Where parenting is involved, the best interests of the child usually coincide with the best interests of the family, too. Starting families with two parents and keeping those parents together through the challenges of married life have to again become an expectation of society. Children of single-parent homes face so many additional risks of poverty and social challenges compared to children of two parent families. The cost to those children, the single parent and ultimately to society make this a crisis that must be addressed.

So while you may be tempted to keep your family contacts to the necessary holiday gatherings and state occasions like weddings and funerals, invest your time and energy into your larger family group.

With more and more digital records becoming available, it is possible for many people to discover more about their family history. Learning about that past may give you some clues about your own patterns of life. Maybe you will see a trend on risk-taking or occupations that are part of your story. Having that long-term context is always useful in keeping perspective in a time of crisis when we feel like we are the first one to face it. Remembering our roots reminds us of our ability to be survivors who succeeded against the odds as our ancestors did.

If life is a collection of our stories, our larger family connections (including those added through marriages) enrich our lives with new stories to share. We can learn a great deal about the ups and downs of life – and how to survive them – by our shared experiences in an extended family. Developing these relationships creates the opportunity to ask for advice and perspective along the way. It also is valuable for your children as they learn about the similar and different paths chosen by ancestors and contemporary family members.

So the next time there is a family gathering opportunity – take it rather than find that creative excuse to pass on the event. It is a good investment!

# HAVING FUN

A balanced life includes many things. It might surprise you to learn that having fun is actually a good investment, too.

We may have the image of the stoic, miserly Scrooge as typical persona of the successful investor.

As we discussed in earlier chapters, our goal is not to have a huge bank account but rather to be truly wealthy in the fullest sense of the word. We can start being wealthy when our bank account is small if we make the right choices. More often than not, our bank account will follow the good choices made in our total experience. A wealthy person has a value that is more than just the number on a balance sheet or income statement, as good as those things can be.

There is an art to having fun that can be understood by the poorest among us and can elude those who seem to have it all. Like so much in life, having fun is a choice. Most anything we can do or go through can be a horrible experience or a pleasant one. We can choose to be positive as we approach any situation, and while that may not solve every problem, it makes solving any problem a more positive experience.

So much of what we can look back on as fun involves relationships. Whether that is the joy of being with friends, experiencing competition in a sport or the shared discovery of a beautiful place, we want to share it with someone else. FaceBook, Twitter, Pinterest, YouTube, Farmville and much of the social media is a way for people to share their experiences. It is more fun to be "with" others.

Many people who aspire to make money believe that life is a serious business with little time for unproductive relationships or activities. They even have a phrase for it – "down time" – to describe what we are losing when we are not working hard.

Of course, life is a balance in this area, too. All play is not productive. But as you can observe in the lives of highly focused workaholics, all work is not productive, either. We need to have time to relax, reflect and share experiences with others, which will in turn give our lives meaning.

Some of these experiences can be in our solitude. To read a book, sit in a garden, mediate/pray, or walk in the woods can be highly gratifying and can help us to decompress.

People who concentrate only on making the next buck never achieve the levels of creativity and perspective that can make them truly productive as human beings.

It also comes back to a sense of purpose in life. If our life is centered on only making more money, the answer to the question, "How much is enough?" always is: "A little more."

Great social gatherings – a "shaboo," as they are sometimes called – are times when you can become one of the many. It might be a community festival, a sporting event or some other celebration of life. Rather than trying to find your meaning in isolation, discover what it means to be in community. Shaboo on!

So resist the temptation to make fun something you will get around to in your golden years. The years you have now are your golden years. Spend them well on your children, your parents and your grandchildren. Invest them in the lives of your faith community, your neighbours, coaching a sports team or volunteering in your town.

As the poet reminds us, we pass this way but once. Take time to enjoy the wonder of the world around us. Then when you are back at the business of making money, you will have the extra energy and perspective of someone who can not only work hard, but play hard, too.

# SALUD!

It has been said that if you don't have your health, you don't have anything. That, of course, is not true. Many people suffering from chronic diseases and other conditions contribute a great deal to our society. Many who are perfectly healthy have little impact in the lives of others.

That being said, it is a good thing for us to be as healthy as possible in the lifestyles we choose. For some of us, this is easier than others. Your health is a combination of what you eat, the genes you inherited, the family health patterns growing up, your culture, life experiences like playing sports and being active, as well as whatever random injuries and diseases you contract over your lifetime. Where you live is also a big factor. There are "healthier" communities in which patterns of behaviour, levels of pollution and even the weather can promote or hinder our health.

It is a fact that it is more expensive to be healthy. Buying higher-quality fresh food is more expensive than the highly processed foods that are available in bulk.

Of course, healthy choices at any stage of our life is really an investment. Eventually, poor health choices that might have been cheaper in the short term catch up with us when we experience chronic diseases that are associated with unhealthy choices. Beyond those direct costs are the lost productivity when we are sick or not able to give our best in our work. The goal is not just health, but true wellness. Preventing injury and disease is always better than the difficulty of doing battle with it.

We live in a time when more is known about the human body and diseases than at any time in history. Yet, many people struggle to be healthy.

Obesity is clearly one of the greatest concerns of our time. What can we do? No universal 12-step program works for everyone. The billions of dollars being spent by people on the myriad of weight-loss solutions who remain overweight demonstrates the complexity of the problem. It is more than just calories and exercise for most people who struggle. It may be that not only our genetics but also our environment is a risk factor in our weight. That along with calories, exercise, social habits, the presence of inflammation, sleeping patterns, aging, depression and so much more can influence this area of life.

Food engages so many emotional and physical responses. Very ancient patterns of stress and survival are engaged in what and how often we eat. It is associated with our childhood experiences, our sense of well-being and even security. Different cultural experiences impact our view of food. It also varies widely depending on our metabolism, hormones and even personality types.

Perhaps we will look back on this period as the final chapter of the problems associated with being overweight as science unlocks this complicated syndrome. What is clear is that the shame-based approach advocated and practiced by many who just cannot understand why someone else can be overweight will be counter-productive.

A starting point where everyone can begin is with the choices relating to the type, quality and quantities of food we eat. That is where most people can begin on the journey. Add to that supportive relationships in your family, friends, health professionals or coaches and you have the beginnings of change that can become a lifestyle that is sustainable.

There are many new supplements based on insights about preventing disease. In the resources section of this book, we recommend that you explore four areas of special interest to staying healthy. The first is understanding pain. So many health problems go back to the onset of pain conditions as we age and through injuries accumulated over our lifetime. Pain specialist Dr. Blair Lamb, M.D., is someone who has revolutionized the way we look at what causes chronic pain and the treatment options available to return to a healthier you.

Another area to understand is the importance of balanced hormones for women and men. Hormones play such an important role in our health patterns, and yet most of us do not know much about whether we are in balance. Changes in hormone levels over our lifetimes including menopause and andropause (male menopause) can impact our heart health, stamina and many other aspects of our healthy lifestyle. Dr. Larry Komer, M.D., makes important contributions to our understanding of healthy hormones.

Gaining a new understanding about brain health is also of key importance. This includes both positive steps we can take to have healthy and active brains over our lifetime. It also deals with the importance of understanding how dangerous concussions are with all of the changes in the body that they trigger. The Traumatic Brain Injury Clinic in Ontario is making an important contribution to the understanding and treatment of those suffering concussions and more.

Pharmacies with healthcare professionals who are committed to improving our health are another underutilized piece of the healthcare puzzle. We highlight the work of pharmacies such as York Downs Pharmacy in Toronto as an example of a place where the wide range of resources for a healthy life are available. Included in these highly valuable pharmacy teams are not only products, but education, as well. In a great return to what is old is new again, some of these pharmacies are compounding pharmacies where required medicines can be customized to the special needs of individuals in the way a product is delivered into the body or the strength or dosage that is ideal for different needs beyond the standard manufactured drugs.

Related to the choices we make in our physical health, it is also important to make healthy choices for the emotional, mental and spiritual dimensions of who we are as people. All of these attitudes and value systems contribute to a healthier future for all of us. The YouTube video "The Seven Vitalities of Life and How Your Pharmacy Can Help" is a wonderful introduction to this.

Exploring healthy relationships and your spiritual development will give you a sense of peace and wellness that is often compromised by conflict and despair.

Your health and the health of those you love is an important investment. So, here is a toast to your health.

Cheers!

Salud!

# HOW LONG DO YOU HAVE?

Many people use online dating services to try to find the perfect match for their most important relationship.

Surveys include your values, your priorities, your interests, your personality and your lifestyle. Through the magic of a large database and wonderful algorithms, many people use these services to help them find a friend who might become more than that.

Finding the right investments also include some of these same matching skills. How much risk are you comfortable taking? How much should be invested in stocks or bonds or real estate or gold or... Ugh! It is complicated!

One of the matching factors that help us sort out the right mix of investment in creating a financial plan is to look at your time frames. What money will you need when?

How long before you need a new car? When will the roof need to be replaced on your house? How long before your children are going to university? When do you want to pay off your mortgage? When will you retire?

Anything you expect to need in the next couple of years needs to be in an investment that has little downside. You will not have the same growth potential as other investments might, but something like a money market fund gives you some return on your money with the liquidity to get your money out in a hurry when you need it.

If your money is for ten years or more, you might consider a growth investment that will have its ups and downs over the short term but usually is up when you are likely to want to cash it in. Some money might not be expected to be needed until retirement. If that is a long way off, you want those dollars to be working hard for you in a long-term growth investment. If you need income from your investment, there are a number of options. You can have either a predictable income stream or a variable income with some growth potential.

These are just some of the planning decisions that we all must make. The alternative is to live from crisis to crisis. A crisis is almost always many times more expensive to solve than the same problem that had a planned solution before it was an emergency.

If you are not good at this (or if you are good at avoiding this!), then using a planning professional can help you get a realistic view of where you are and what you will need when in the future.

# STABLE VS. SAFE

One of the many contradictions we experience in life is the difference between what is stable and what is safe. For many people, these could be synonyms. Stability is safety. Safety is stability. Or is it?

Change is hard. Living through the changes that have been normal for the past three generations is unprecedented. So much of what we know now was unknown a hundred years ago. Many things we take for granted were ideas of science fiction fifty years ago. We know that many of the devices and technologies that we are using now will be obsolete in a few years. We expect change.

The kind of massive changes that everyone faces now can make us long for an "easier time" when life was simpler. Change happened slowly, if at all. This makes it great for people who sell nostalgia or for producers of the wonderful period pieces depicting the last couple of centuries. In fact, life was full of challenges of a different type in the not-too-distant past. Change was happening then, too.

Whatever your experience with change may be, you develop a feeling of what is normal. If change happens faster than that, then you feel the stress of change. We all do not handle change at the same level. It is similar to what constitutes "rush hour" in your community. Many towns have very slow traffic at certain times of day as people come and go for work. The peak rush hour might last thirty minutes in one community. The distance from work to home might be fifteen minutes. That becomes normal. Take that person and land them into life in one of the major cities where it is easier to describe when it is not rush hour and commutes are measured in hours per day, and they would be very stressed. It is far beyond what is their normal experience. Of course, the reverse is also true. Take someone from the major cities and move them to a smaller city. They will find it difficult to describe rush hour in that new community by comparison.

In the world of investments, the same is true. We all have different tolerances for change – or to use the term we use in finance, risk. The two ends of the teeter-totter for most investors are safety and risk. Will my investment be safe? What are the risks?

What we mean by that is usually: How certain will I be that the money I put in will be there when I want to take it out? A secondary thought will be: How certain will I be of the earnings I hope to receive?

This makes our seesaw have safety and stability on one side, with risk and change on the other side. Particularly after crashes of the stock market, we want our world to be heavily on the safety side of the balance.

The contradiction is that the most stable investments may not be truly safe, depending on your definition of what is safe.

If "safe" means unchanging or predictable, the most conservative investments are appealing because they are stable.

But what does it really mean to have a safe retirement fund or investment of any kind? In very simple terms, we want to be able to buy as much or more with our money in the future. If we are not spending it on something today, we want our money to be able to buy what we need in the future when we do want or need to spend it. That takes a different calculation.

As discussed elsewhere in this book, we want to know not just how much we will "make," but how much we will "keep" in the end. That means that we need to understand what we have after taxes and after inflation. Taxes are easier to see right away. Your income from investments may be taxed very differently depending on whether it is interest, dividend or capital gains income. That has to be part of your strategy. The other question is inflation. There are periods of time when inflation is low. Other times, inflation chews away at our purchasing power at a faster pace. Many can remember the periods when super inflation meant that prices were rising every week or two. During those times, you would hear about how painful inflation was for those on a "fixed" income. Those were the people who had the same amount of money coming in but could not buy the same amount of groceries, housing or other necessities.

The people on a fixed income had "stable" income. They knew what they were going to earn. But they did not have a "safe" income because it was not giving them the same ability to maintain their lifestyle year after year.

Safe investments include the right combination of risk and reward that will achieve your goals after taxes and after inflation. Your investment adviser or bank adviser will help you find the best combination of investments that will achieve your goals over the time you will keep your money invested. For everyone, that is a different combination depending on your age, plans and comfort level. Great planning is the best way to achieve the rewards for putting your money to work.

Do not settle for "stable," no matter how tempting certainty seems to be.

It is not the safe move.

# TAKE IT TO THE BANK

Banks have enjoyed a love-hate relationship with the public. The endless series of charges and fees seems to drain off so much of our everyday money. So many of them seem not only too big to fail, but too big to care about us as individuals. It seems like one of those relationships that we cannot live with or live without.

If that is your feeling about all banks, it is time to do some homework. More and more banks are reaching out to develop your financial future, combining a range of services that go beyond simple savings, a car loan and a mortgage. Many banks now offer a wide range of investment services to meet the full-service needs of investors, as well.

Some of this is due to competitive pressures by trust companies and credit unions. Most of it comes from the regulatory changes that give banks a wider role in our financial life.

This is the right time to develop a relationship with your banker.

Most people are afraid to discuss their finances with others – even those who are in the business to help you with them. Some of this is from a sense of inadequacy. You can always imagine a richer person coming in to speak to them. You might not trust them if you have had difficulties in the past.

What the current bankers can do for you is quite amazing. They have divisions that handle clients at different wealth levels, so do not worry about what you have or have not got at the present. What they want to do is create a relationship with you that leads you to do your investing and borrowing with them in the future. They know that many people will accumulate their wealth over a period of decades. Banks are okay with that. They are in it for the long term. They see each relationship as a possibility to develop over time. Some will be average. Some will not do so well. Some will be very successful. The banks are big enough to take those risks because you might be one of those average clients where they do well. You might also become one of those wealthy clients where you all do very well.

Approach your prospective banker much as you would when you are buying a new car. What features do they offer? What services do they include to keep you rolling along? What kind of relationship will they develop to help you through the bad times and the good ones?

Get their advice on the kind of plan that suits your goals and time frames. That can include borrowing and investing. They will offer advice on how to move forward in a way that matches your objectives.

The best part of this is that their advice is usually included within the cost of the loan or the investment. Such a deal.

Keep checking with your sage or other financial friend to share perspectives on how the advice you are receiving will truly help.

But do not overlook the option of receiving the advice and support from your personal banking representative as you move forward.

# RAINY DAYS

Some people love a rainy day. It can be a nice change from a streak of hot, steamy days. In the financial world, a "rainy day" is a very bad thing. Something has happened unexpectedly that has stopped us in our tracks. Instead of the sunny days when all is going well, the storms of a rainy day suggest risk and danger. That is why we set aside money for a "rainy day fund" to help us get through a time when we have unexpected expenses or a loss of income due to changes in our health or employment.

Traditionally, the amount we should have in our emergency reserves is equal to three months of income. That gives you some flexibility to deal with unexpected short-term changes in life. Other decisions would have to be made if the challenge is going to last longer than this. If your income goes up and down through different seasons or depends on sales, then your three-month calculation should be from your best three months of income – not an average three.

You may want to have a larger emergency reserve if you know that you have some of your major repairs or replacements coming due soon. If your roof is starting to show wear and tear, start setting aside money for the repair sooner rather than later. A leaky roof can do much more damage and end up becoming a much larger expense than if you can fix it at the time it needs repair or replacement. Similarly, if you know that your car will need a new set of tires before next winter, make sure that the extra money is in your reserves.

These emergency funds should be somewhere that you can access quickly. That could be a money market fund (treasury bills, etc.) or a savings account at the bank. This will not give you the same potential upside return as other investments, but the rainy day fund is investing in peace of mind. It is stressful to live knowing that at any moment, something could go wrong and you would have no way to solve it financially.

As in the case of the roof above, do not let your rainy day fund keep you from being proactive on spending money to repair or replace items before they become a crisis. It is a much easier repair for a roof if it is a clear, sunny day than a bitter winter storm.

If you think about your family finances as a small business, you need those cash reserves just as any business would. There are always unexpected expenses no matter how well you plan. So, plan for the unplanned. It will help you reduce your expenses over the long term, and it will help you have a better night's rest when that rainy day finally arrives.

# INSURE TO BE SURE

Certainty is something people have always longed to have as part of their life. If only I knew for sure, then I could make good decisions. Life has always been uncertain. For the generations of the past, it was uncertainty caused by failing crops, pestilence, epidemics, weather and wars. As you read through history, it is amazing that any of us survived! As we look at some of the most challenged places in our current world, we wonder how anyone there could possible survive.

We still face many uncertainties in our time. Weather can bring flooding and other kinds of destruction. Disease can impact large groups as well as individuals. Accidents happen every day. Jobs can disappear. Markets rise and fall. People die unexpectedly. What can we do with all of the uncertainties that are part of life?

That is the role of insurance. Matching the right kind of insurance to your risks is part of any good financial plan. Too much insurance can make you insurance poor. Not enough insurance can leave your loved ones in need.

What should you know about life insurance?

Many books have been written about life insurance. It is an important topic to learn as much as you can about. Financial and insurance professionals will be able to review what is appropriate for your particular circumstances. But here are some of the big ideas to grasp.

Life insurance is temporary. Life insurance is to cover your liabilities and to provide an income for those who depend on you until you no longer have liabilities and there are enough assets to cover the needs of your dependents. Get as much life insurance as you need to leave your dependents with no debt and the ability to earn enough income from what is left to keep them living as before.

Life insurance is not a saving vehicle. Do not confuse savings or investing with your life insurance. Term life insurance gives you the purest form of life insurance at the lowest cost for as long as you need it. When you do not need it, you stop buying it.

If you can buy your term life insurance as part of your employment or by belonging to a group, that often reduces the cost of the monthly premiums. Make sure that the insurance will not stop with your employment or membership in the group.

Some kinds of life insurance combine a savings or investment product with the insurance. It is usually sold on the idea that you will have something left at the end. That usually means that you have to pay much more for the same insurance coverage each month. Do not worry about "cash value" from a life insurance policy. That would be like paying much more for your auto insurance each month so that you would have something at the end whether or not you had a car accident. Life insurance is to cover your dependents if you die before you have no debt, enough investments to pay a regular income or no dependents. If you can outlive your need for life insurance, you already succeeded! Keep your investments and your insurance as separate concepts.

(I know that there are strategies that use whole life insurance, which can be used as a tax planning tool for estates to pay forward on taxes. That can be useful for passing down a family cottage, etc., but that is a different purpose than life insurance to allow a grieving family to continue as before.)

Other types of insurance to consider include disability insurance. This helps pay the bills if you can no longer work due to accident or illness. This is especially important if we end up with a long-term disability rather than just being ill or unable to work for a short period of time in which our emergency savings can keep us going.

Speak to your insurance and financial guides to learn more and to find the right amount of coverage that you can afford each month that will care for your loved ones if you face long-term disability or if you die.

# CAN I BORROW THAT?

An excellent credit rating can be one of your most important assets. Those with a good credit rating can borrow at a lower cost and with more flexibility than those with a poor credit score. Talk with your banker or other financial adviser about what you can do to build up and keep a great credit rating. In simple terms, people with the best credit ratings pay back what they borrow at least as fast as their minimum payments allow. They usually do not borrow to the maximum of their financial capability. Strange as it seems, it is even better if you borrow money without needing to due to the assets that you already have.

When should you borrow?

Borrowing makes sense for many people if they are purchasing an appreciating asset. We usually associate this with getting a mortgage to buy a house. History teaches us that while real estate often appreciates over time, it does not always go up. Even when it is going up in one part of the country, it can go down somewhere else at the same time. This becomes a problem if the amount you agree to pay on a floating interest rate mortgage each month rises with interest rates so that you can not make your payments. If you have a fixed payment schedule, you have greater certainty on your payments but you are still at risk if you lose your job or your expenses go up in other areas. That is why it is a good idea not to borrow more than you can comfortably afford to repay each month.

The banks and other lenders have ratios that they use to calculate how much of your income is available for your loan payments and therefore how large your loan will be. That number in combination with how much cash you have saved to put as a down payment on your house will determine the price of the house you can afford. Many people become overly optimistic about how much and how fast their house price might go up. That leads them to buy more house than they can truly afford. It will make them "mortgage poor" as they pay too large a percentage of their income to the loan, not leaving them enough to have a balanced life. That is a huge source of stress for many people.

Other loans people make can involve home renovations. Some projects tend to add value to your house, while others may not. Talk to your trusted realtor to find out whether you are adding value to just taking a loan for something you might enjoy.

Car loans are tricky because you are borrowing for a depreciating item. (Cars lose value each year, with new cars losing the most as soon as your car goes from new to used – as you drive it off the lot!) For many people, a car is vital to your work or other commitments you have. Not all communities have robust public transportation to get you where you want to go. If you do need to borrow for your car, put as much money down as you can and only borrow what you need to in order to get the car. For people who use their car for business, there may be tax planning reasons to finance your car rather than buy it for cash. In many cases, a pre-owned car may give you a better value if you can purchase it reliably, since the car has already been depreciated from when it was new. Do your homework on the reliability and typical resale values of the car you select.

Student loans are often the first experience that most people have with debt. Treat these commitments seriously, as they will affect your credit rating. As with all loans, work to pay them off sooner than necessary, since those extra monthly dollars available after the loan is paid can move you forward to the next level.

If you run into financial problems and know that you are going to have a problem making your payments, contact your lender right away. Explain the situation. If it is a temporary blip, they will work with you to try to get through the problem. If it is a long-term change, then you need to have the courage to make the difficult choices. Do not ignore financial problems as they keep on growing.

Before taking out or renewing a loan, talk to your financial adviser to look at all of the options available to you. There are different ways to secure loans that can be at a lower interest rate.

Loans are an excellent reason to have insurance, as discussed elsewhere in the book. Be sure that your debts are covered by insurance or other assets in case you die.

This is another reason to save for an emergency fund that covers 3-6 months of income or expenses. That way, in case you lose your job or face some other crisis that requires money, you will have enough to keep you going.

Good financial planning is the key to good credit.

# PLAYING CARDS

Even before graduation from college and university, most people are offered a credit card. It makes you feel very important and optimistic about your future. This company has sent me a credit card! Wow!! They must know that I am going to be successful in life.

It may be that you will be very successful in life, but the credit card companies do not know that for sure, yet. They may have looked at the fact that you are studying at a post-secondary institution and feel that you are a good risk. Just as importantly, they believe that if they become "your card" now, then they will likely have you for life.

Credit cards can be very useful tools in your financial toolbox. The ability to rent a car or do the host of other transactions is a real plus. The credit card became very important to the health of the economy because that meant spending more today than you have. If you cannot pay off the full balance by the date in your agreement, then you will also have to pay interest. The credit card company loves interest payments – that is part of their profit every day.

If you are like most people, you will probably have approaches from the department stores and gas cards first. They are willing to take a bigger risk that someone will not ultimately be able to pay in part because they earn more when you purchase something at their store or when you fill up your tank. The general bank credit cards are more conservative, priced at better interest rates for ongoing balances, and usually require a solid job in addition to just having prospects. The advantage of the general bank credit card is that the interest rates are often much better than those of a store card. You do not need to be store-specific.

Credit cards are a business transaction first and foremost. They come with higher rates of interest than other loans because they are not typically secured by an asset or investment. Therefore, there is a higher level of risk for the bank or card issuer. The higher the risk that people will not be able to pay back their debt, the more a lender will charge to account for the added risks involved.

Understand that many cards attract customers with a special rate if you transfer your existing balances into a new card. New "affinity" cards connect you to different incentives for rewards or other benefits. Do not just look at the incentives, but also look at the fees and interest rates on the cards you are considering. Also, be aware that you may be offered a low interest rate for a specific period of time and then find yourself with much higher interest costs down the road.

Do not let the emotional inducements or the flattery of being offered a card when you have no money entice you into a long-term challenge.

Used wisely, a credit card can be a useful tool. Beware of the trap of using it to finance a future you are not ready to pay for today.

This is an area in which your financial counsellors can really help you in making the best choices as to what card you choose and how you use it along the way.

# THE KEYS

Cars are one of the early investments for most people. It might be a joint venture with your parents or a purchase you make from your savings. It may be a choice you defer until after university or even into later life if you live and work in an area that includes excellent mass transit and friendly bike lanes. For many others, a car is essential for work as well as play. It may be one of those dreams of your early journey.

Unlike many other purchases, buying a car has very high emotional content involved in the decision-making process. This is not a bad thing – but you do need to be aware of it all through the stages of considering if, when and what car you purchase. There is a reason why parents and grandparents talk about their first car as a long-lost first love. Many highly charged elements go into that first automotive relationship. Owning your first car is a step toward independence. It is a status symbol. It is a statement about your personal preferences (or the inability financially to express them) as you choose older or newer cars with more or less of the features available. In recent years, you also have a green element to what you purchase, which says something about your view of climate change and society.

Whenever you get to it, there are some big ideas to consider.

First, cars are a depreciating investment. That means that as you own it and use it over time, it is dropping in value. Two major factors influence the future value. One is the age of the car, and the other is the mileage. The newer the car and the lower the mileage, the more value it will hold. The other factor that you can influence less is how popular and desirable the particular year and model of your car are for those wishing to own it.

You can slow the rate of decline in the car's value by taking good care of it, regularly maintaining it with your automotive specialist. Another way to reduce the depreciation is to buy a reliable used car, since as soon as a car goes from "new to used," it may lose anywhere up to 25-35% of its value as you drive it off the new car dealer's lot.

If you choose to own your car immediately by paying for it, you will eliminate the interest costs associated with a loan. But you will also have taken away whatever growth potential was there for those dollars that might have been saved or invested for the future. As with many financial decisions, there is no absolute right or wrong here for everyone. It is a series of choices that will change the way your future unfolds. It is as simple and complex as our three S chapter.

Other cost issues include insurance, how fuel efficient the vehicle is, what the maintenance expenses will be and even the speed at which you drive. If you are going to own a car, start by learning about it. Ask questions of family and friends to learn what you should know. Then talk to your financial and insurance advisers about your ideas. Make sure that your trusted mechanic meets your car. He should inspect it before you commit to the purchase.

So as you fall in love with that first car with all of the imperfections and challenges that you will experience together, be sure that you have saved up enough money to take it out for a drive without worrying about how much money is left for the drive-in.

# YOUR CASTLE

There was a time when castles had similar designs for their times. Now your castle might be anything from a suburban home, a place in the country, an apartment downtown, an old family farm, a condo, a trailer, a grand estate or something in between. It might be a purchased place, or perhaps you are renting.

As the old adage suggests, it is the place we call home that makes a place your castle.

Finding and deciding about the place you will call home is a series of big decisions. As many people found out after a housing bubble, owning your home is not always the best choice financially, even if it seems like the only dream we can imagine. Others despair that the high cost of renting means that they will never be able to save enough money for the down payment of the house they wish to buy because the prices keep rising faster than the savings.

Whether you are ready for the cost of purchasing AND maintaining a house with all of the taxes involved is a decision that needs to combine both courage and wisdom. It is easy to believe that you can make it work by cutting out everything else in your life or by taking a second job. Wisdom includes having a realistic sense of what you can reliably earn and save over a five-year period of time. Seeking advice from bankers and other financial advisers during this process who will be honest with you is crucial. If they tell you that you are not yet in a strong enough position to make the purchase, have the courage to continue saving and renting. If they say that it is time to move into home ownership, do your homework and then have the courage to make that big move.

Generally, the closer you are to the big city (if it is healthy) with the shortest commute, the more expensive your house will be to purchase or rent. Take an identical house and move it further away, and it will tend to be less expensive. The trade-off is that dreaded word – commuting. Understand that what you save in money for your purchase is an exchange with the cost of transportation and, even more importantly, your time. If you can work from home or have flexible hours, then those can make the commuting less of a factor.

Balancing of the cost of your housing, the cost of your transportation and the time spent on the road are all key in the decision of where to locate your home base.

What many people discover over their lifetimes is that some of their happiest memories happened in their less-than-ideal home settings. You may have had too many people for the size of a house. The apartment may have been full of the odors of many different cultures cooking down the hall, above and below you. The elevators were terribly slow, or the house had an old furnace system that had a personality of its own. As with much of life, how we adapt to the challenging times makes up part of the tales that enrich our life stories.

No matter where your home circumstances are, you will be adding to the chapters of your life while you are there. It might be your first place on your own. Perhaps it is your first place as a couple. Children may learn to walk while you are there. Pay attention to what is happening where you live as you go through your days at your castle. Ask the walls what they observed today. They will have some good stories to tell – if you could only get them to talk.

# PROTECTING YOUR CASTLE

Being an optimistic person does not insulate you from the life experiences that happen to everyone sooner or later. Whether you rent or own your house, it is very important to have enough of the right kind of renter's or homeowner's insurance.

One of the advantages that experienced insurance brokers and agents have is that they have witnessed some of the strangest things that could happen in an apartment or home. If you want a good story, ask them about some of the weird things that they have encountered.

We often think of the obvious risks of fire and basements flooding. There is wind damage, damage caused by something falling on your house like a tree. If the power fails, all sorts of problems can happen from frozen pipes that burst to freezers full of food spoiling. Even similar events like water in your basement can have different insurance issues depending on whether the water came through the foundation or from a burst pipe or from a backed-up sewer.

Liability insurance for your property is also important since someone visiting or working on your property might slip and fall. Injuries can happen to adults or children. It is difficult enough to deal with the human dimension of accidents without also having the financial impact, as well.

If you are in a condominium or other multi-unit property, something going wrong can quickly become someone else's problem if water from your unit leaks into that person's unit. It also matters whether someone else who causes damage to your property has insurance to cover damage to you.

The range of things that can go wrong takes several books to discuss. The big idea that I want you to catch here is that renter's and homeowner's insurance is comparatively inexpensive. That is because like all insurance covering groups of people in similar circumstances, there is a shared risk that reduces the cost. Thankfully, most people do not have a claim very often on their property. That also reduces the risk and therefore the cost.

I always recommend meeting with your insurance brokers or agents to discuss the full range of coverage available to you. It is amazing how much more can be covered for a few extra dollars a month. Get your insurance professional to educate you on what their "sleep well" policy is that covers the typical problems that end up keeping renters and homeowners up after a disaster strikes. Especially focus on what kind of flood insurance you might need for the various kinds of water damage that can happen. Ask what the experience is for people in your area with water and wind damage to ensure that you have what you need. Be sure you have the liability insurance you might reasonably need. Find out what your responsibilities are to keep your insurance in full force, such as having working smoke detectors or a functioning sump-pump.

Do not skimp on your renter's or homeowner's insurance. Sleep well!

# BUYING A CASTLE

Real estate is a fact of life – and terror for most people. Sooner or later you will engage in the quest for something that uniquely involves as much about emotions as it does making a rational decision.

As discussed earlier, you first need to know whether you are financially ready to make a purchase. That involves your savings, your income and job stability, and your plans concerning how long you will stay in that house. Generally, you want to plan to be in your house for at least five years in order to allow for the ups and downs of the real estate market. There are also the costs of selling and moving into a different house, including real estate fees, taxes and moving expenses. Any move has to either be necessary for your job or family needs or should be able to justify the cost of selling and buying.

As a rule, real estate has been a good investment over time if you are living near a growing community with solid employment and favourable reasons to live there. A quick look at those conditions helps you realize why real estate is not always a great short-term investment. Recessions, loss of employment, high taxes and many other factors can scare away potential buyers from your area. If people do not want to move to your area, your real estate values are susceptible to not growing or to going down.

Some communities are influenced by industries that go up and down with demand in the economy. Cities that are built on the car industry will see their wealth and employment go up and down with sales of their brand of vehicle. If industries begin to be moved to other countries, real estate values tend to stay down or decline for long periods of time. Some communities are part of the boom and bust of commodities like oil or mining. When prices of the commodities are up – so is real estate. At other times, they can face sharp declines. Border cities or tourist towns can also go up and down depending on whether people are coming to spend their money where you live. Changing demographics also matter. If your community is not attracting younger families, chances are the upward pressure on values will start to disappear and prices will no longer go up. The cost of commuting also can make your bedroom community too expensive to choose because of the price of gas to get to the big city where the jobs are. It is a complicated decision.

Real estate has also been one of the sectors of the economy in which there have been many booms and busts. Less reputable real estate agents will tend to minimize the risks involved since their role is to get the sale done – whether you are the buyer or seller. Better agents will help you evaluate the factors in your decision. They also will steer you away from buying when the market is at a high or from buying more house than you can afford if times suddenly get tough.

Look for real estate professionals who can give you many references from people who have used them over the years. They are more likely to give you the quality advice you will need. Include your banker, financial advisers and trusted family or friends for the perspective you need. Remember, your home tends to be your largest single investment. Invest well!

# IMPROVING YOUR CASTLE

Whether you go the contractor or DIY route, most of us will end up changing the way our castle was when we bought it.

You can watch the many renovation shows on television to see the range of success and horror stories people experience when trying to make their homes a bit better or bigger.

The most important decision you can make in the renovation process is to take your time.

That starts with taking time to plan. Think through what you are actually trying to accomplish with the changes. Is it to add value for resale? If so, find out what renovations actually increase the selling price in your area. Are you starting the project to improve your quality of life? If so, you should be able to describe what you want to be different or better when you are done.

If it is a do-it-yourself (DIY) project, be sure to know ALL of the requirements you will face, including getting planning permission, inspections, and what skilled trades will still be needed because of the building code, along with what skills you will need to do your part. Most of us have some handy friends who have done projects – get their help in planning. They are usually happy to give the advice because people who start a DIY project without proper planning end up calling those same friends to bail them out of a disaster. Many large DIY stores now will provide training and support for specific types of projects. Plan. Plan. Plan! Take the time to do it.

If you are using contractors, you again want to do the full review of all of the decisions you will face. Make the plan carefully, since changing partway through usually becomes very expensive once you have begun the project. Get a budget that involves all of the labour and materials. Include a quote for how changes will be charged if they are made. Discuss how payments are to be made. Do not get too far ahead of paying for work that is not done. Do not get too far behind either, or your contractor will focus on where the money is flowing. Check references from the contractor.

Be wary of contractors who want cash payments to "save the tax," as that usually makes you more vulnerable to resolving problems since the "under the table" trades also do not belong to the Better Business Bureau or other professional organizations. Besides all of that, "saving them the tax" takes money out of our communities for healthcare, police, fire and other services paid for with our tax dollars. You usually will not realize the level of savings promised, since if it was dollar-for-dollar, why would they not want to pay the taxes involved? There is usually more to the story and less to the contractor when they start the relationship by inviting you to do something illegal.

Depending on the size of your renovation, you may wish to engage a project manager who will supervise the trades to ensure that the project is on time and on budget.

Always allow more time than planned for your renovation. Always have extra money available in case the project goes over budget. There is nothing worse than living in an unfinished project.

A renovation can be a smart investment that can increase the value of your castle and can make the castle that much more of a pleasant place in which to live. Whether it is a contractor or DIY, make sure it is a DIAP – Did It As Planned – to make it a pleasant tale rather than a horror story.

# SELLING YOUR CASTLE

To sell the family home can be a time full of many mixed emotions. There are many reasons why it may be time to sell.

Sometimes, selling your home is triggered by a change of employment. The need to live in a different town or city because of a new or different job usually comes down to the hassle of a move versus how feasible it is to continue to live where you are with the added commute.

A growing family may require an extra bedroom or more space for the family to use for everyday life. A generation or two ago, it was not uncommon for the ebb and flow of growing and graduating children to cause a change in sharing rooms or installing bunk beds rather than moving to a larger house. Now, it is common for people to move up to larger homes two or three times as their family grows.

At the other end of the aging process, the reverse cycle begins with empty nesters looking at their larger unused house and sizing down to a smaller home or a condo. Many couples and individuals follow that with a move to either a seniors community or smaller town. Live long enough, and you may move to a seniors retirement housing. Sometimes the health needs of one or more of the family members trigger these changes. Other times, it is a loss of a spouse that brings about the sale.

Most homes accumulate a wealth of memories from your years there. "If these walls could talk!" usually expresses the range of feelings associated with our time in a particular place. We have joys and sorrows associated with that property. Children may have learned to walk there, and as with life, sadness and pain are usually represented by the times passed in that place. For children and for the elderly, a move is especially difficult. It often reflects uncertainty about the future for the children who cannot imagine a different bedroom or making new friends. An uncomfortable certainty awaits the senior who is experiencing another of the diminishing list of life experiences that still await them.

When a move is under way, it is important to include the emotional cost in the decision.

As discussed earlier, identifying a responsive and experienced real estate agent who will work *with* you as well as *for* you to sell your house for the best price and in the best time frame that meets your needs is essential.

Beware of the agent who concentrates only on the sale, since the agent's commission is a similar dollar amount whether the sale maximizes the value of the property or represents something closer to a fire sale. Talk to your financial advisers about what is happening in your real estate market so that you can price your property to sell for the best price in the time you have available.

If you are selling your home and buying another, be sure to look at the implications of moving up to a more expensive house in a down market versus an up market. If you are doing the reverse, be careful to time your selling of the more expensive house as you buy a less expensive home or condominium as your next place to live. It can make a big difference in your strategy and your long-term wealth position.

# CASTLES BY THE SEA

The opportunity to have a vacation property creates some great opportunities for celebration, but it is full of dangers, as well.

Vacation properties can come in a variety of ownership structures. We will look at three of the most common types you are likely to encounter.

The first is when you purchase a cabin or cottage where you own the property independently, much as you would own your house. This gives you the normal benefits and risks of owning real estate. If your home is in a community with a flat history of property values, you might be wise to have less house and more cottage if the long-term trend on your cottage area values are better.

When it is a recreation property like a cottage, you should review with your real estate and financial advisers the trends of recreational properties in the area you are considering. Sometimes, real estate can be doing very well in neighbouring communities but not as well in the recreational areas because of high taxes, costs of transportation, too many recent builds or changing demographics with less interest in cottage ownership. If it is a cottage, do not forget to review any special insurance requirements, since you will not always be at your property or you may rent it out. These all may require special coverage.

Be sure to do your research on the recreation area where you might purchase a cottage. It is also important to see the features, like the swimming area in the summer when it is in use. If you have a mucky or stony bottom as you enter your swimming area, you will not find it as appealing to you or a future purchaser as a soft, sandy bottom with a gradual walk to deeper water. The side of the lake you choose can also matter, as often people prefer sunsets over sunrises. Check out the currents and other features of the lake. Ask what other development is approved or potentially planned as more cottages put more pressure on the lake and its recreation. Connect with a cottage specialist in real estate to help you on the journey.

A second option is that you purchase recreational real estate that is part of an area association where your property is part of a community in which you have shared benefits (like a swimming pool or recreation center) and shared costs that go beyond your purchase cost. Do your homework on how old the common facilities are. Is money set aside by the association each year to improve or replace the aging facilities – or are they just maintaining what is there? Eventually those common features will need to be replaced at the expense of the owners like you. Look for a well-managed group that is planning ahead rather than just paying for today. Ask to see the long-term costs to see what the trends are in the group. You should always have a lawyer review these common agreements in advance of a purchase to know what your potential liabilities are – as well as what controls the association might have over how you enjoy your property.

Another popular way to have a vacation property is through a time-share, in which you own a portion of the property – often with a specified week or weeks when it is your turn to use it. Some time-shares include the ability to exchange your weeks with others in your property. Many are part of larger time-share groups that allow you to exchange your "week" for a comparable time in other properties in North America or around the world. This can be a great way to have a place to go to with a fraction of the cost. It can also be a great way to see different parts of the world if you can afford the transportation to your swapped time-share.

These types of investments require some sales resistance, as many of the properties will invite you up for a free weekend and then use the time to convince you what a great investment it is. If it is a great investment, it will stand up to a review by your financial adviser and your lawyer before you sign on the dotted line. Be suspicious of any place that is rushing you to decide before you can get independent advice. Be sure that you know what it is that you actually own with the investment. Ask what happens if the management group has financial problems. You do not want to own a week in a place that is no longer there.

The "castle by the sea" concept is an old one. It has been a great source of memories and wealth for many people. It can turn into a generational experience as it is shared with family and friends over the years you own it. Discovering what is right for you in your financial circumstances will take some exploring to get it right. That is the best way to have a wonderful place to enjoy when you are away.

# CASTLES FOR RENT

There are times when it makes sense to rent either your home or a vacation property. Many people also purchase income properties as an investment and sail into the adventure of being "the landlord" or "landlady" with all that this represents.

If you are a handy person or one who is patient with people, this might be an opportunity to consider. Many people have added to their wealth over time by owning rental properties. In addition to whatever positive income the property represents, investors hope that the increased value of the real estate will give them an asset to sell at some time down the road.

Between the purchase and the final sale, however, is usually a great deal of work, some times of terror, and typically some unbelievable tenant stories that only other property owners will believe possible. If you are up for that kind of adventure, it may be a good move for you.

There are many factors in selecting the rental property. Are you buying a house that you will rent out with the view of selling it as a residential property later? Are you investing in a multi-unit rental unit? These usually are valued by how much rental income is generated. As you can see already, these are two very different kinds of properties to sell at the end of your ownership. Each will involve a very different strategy when you purchase them and while you own them.

As with any property, if you have shared or common areas in your property that require you to be part of an association, be careful to investigate your obligations. Look for what common areas are your responsibility to support. Ask if some of the common fees are being set aside to update or replace the common swimming pool, tennis court or community room as they age. Facilities that only pay for maintenance often end up looking old sooner than expected, leaving the new owners to have to pay for or finance the upgrades.

Tennant rights vary widely from jurisdiction to jurisdiction. Often neighbouring communities will have different rules that apply. Be sure to learn all you need to know about what you can require from a prospective tenant, what you can charge, how much notice you can give for them to leave, and what your obligations are if they turn out to be a bad tenant. Be sure to speak with a real estate lawyer who is willing to guide you through the minefields of rental properties.

In addition to the tenants, you will need to manage your rental property. That can include everything from finding tenants and collecting rents to paying bills and doing repairs. If you a handy person, you might want to do much of this yourself. But it is usually a different set of skills required to deal with choosing good tenants and dealing with their complaints. Some people use a management company for some or all of this. It may mean less income after expenses, but it can also mean fewer mistakes. One of the most common mistakes is picking a tenant who then refuses to pay or to leave.

Assume that you will have periods of time when you will have a vacant rental unit. Can you carry the costs of the property without rental income each month? These kinds of calculations are important to do with your financial advisers before you purchase a property. A second property can be a great way to add wealth for you and your family. Do yourself the favor of researching carefully before you buy.

# TAKING STOCK

Most people in North America own stock either directly or indirectly. They may have a "portfolio" of stocks made through their retirement account. Others own stock indirectly through mutual funds or through their company or group pension that invests in the stock market.

Very simply, owning a stock is owning part of a company that is usually listed on a stock exchange. That stock will have more or less value depending on the earnings and potential of the company. If it is in a growing area of business or is well run, the stock often goes up. If it is a business area in which there are poor sales or if the company is not well run, it is likely to go down in value.

If it is a positive time for the economy and it looks like most businesses will do better, then most (but not all!) stocks will likely go up. If it looks like stormy weather ahead for the economy, then the markets usually see most (but not all!) stocks go down in value.

This fluctuation is both the excitement and the terror of being invested in the stock market. It appeals to the two big emotions of finances: fear and greed. Too much fear causes investors to miss opportunities. These down markets are called "bear" markets. Markets that continue to rise are known as "bull" markets. Too much greed takes you for a ride on the bubble that can suddenly burst, sending you and your investment on a sharp decline.

This is another area in which financial advice is key. Money invested in stocks usually needs to be able to remain invested for five or ten years to allow it to go through the ups and downs of the marketplace. You do not want to rush in to buy when everyone else is buying. You also do not want to sell your stock when the investment is down, or else you will lock in your losses.

Some stocks (and stock funds) are focused on growth. The advisers choose or recommend stocks that are poised to grow. Often these are smaller companies or companies that need to reinvest what they earn to continue to develop their products or services in order to expand the future potential of the stock.

Other companies have a greater focus on dividends. Dividends are paid out of the earnings of companies, often more established and mature companies. Whether a growth or dividend strategy is best for you depends on many of your financial goals and how comfortable you are with risk.

Another variable is whether your stocks are from companies based in your country alone or from countries listed on international stocks. There are advantages and risks associated with company stocks that are outside your borders.

A good financial adviser will help you with these questions.

# BONDING

Bonds have been a traditional way for people to safely have their investments reduce the downside while earning some interest. Savings bonds are the most common examples of this.

These are often issued by a level of government to borrow money to provide the services and infrastructure for their citizens (and more often to pay for the interest on projects done long ago and never paid for at the time.)

Such a bond might have a fixed rate of interest for a specific time with no change in the starting value (principal) of the bond itself. These investments are as good as the government offering it. Be sure that you have confidence in the entity guaranteeing your investment.

Remember, the measure of how well an investment does is not what you earn but what you keep after tax and inflation. If inflation is higher than the interest rate you are earning each year, then your investment really is losing value each year even though it is paying the interest promised. The disadvantage of this kind of investment is that interest is often taxed at the highest level. On the upside, if stock markets or other investments such as real estate go down, you have limited your risk by not having an investment that fluctuates.

Other kinds of bonds do fluctuate in value. These bonds are what you will hear included with reports on the stock market. They usually are only available in large amounts and have a fixed date when they will be redeemed (like a 30-year or 10-year period) and a specific interest rate associated with them. These bonds are often traded because their value is connected to interest rates. If a bond promised a high rate of interest when it was issued compared to current interest rates, it will be more desirable (valuable) than current bonds at the low rates. The opposite is true if the bond was offering lower rates than you could receive on a new bond. Investors will prefer the new bonds and not give you as much (discount) for the older bonds. On longer-term bonds such as a 30-year bond, you are not just comparing current interest rates but also what you think the rates might be over the life of the bond.

Sound complicated? These longer bonds are compared to the basic savings bonds. You may have money invested in the longer bonds through a mutual fund or pension fund, so do not be surprised if you too are James or Jane Bond, too.

# THE FEELING IS MUTUAL

One of the strategies used by many people to invest is mutual funds, in which investments are shared. This can be a great way to get started investing for the future as well as building your portfolio as you grow.

One of the important principles of investing is diversification. It is that old proverb about not putting all of your eggs in one basket. If you invest your money in one company and that company does well, then you are happy. If that one company does not do well, then your investment is in trouble. It is better to have a diversified portfolio that includes investments chosen to give you the best upside potential with the lowest downside risk. For individuals to purchase shares from a combination of companies, it usually requires a great deal of money because of the minimum costs of doing stock trades in which you buy or sell a share. If you do not have a great deal of money to invest, you often will not be able to get the best advice about where and when to invest your money.

A mutual fund solves a number of these problems. It is a way for a large pool of investors to own a wider range of investments than they could easily do as individuals. Most investment funds allow you to invest a minimum of a thousand dollars, which buys "units" in the fund. The way the unit value is calculated is to take all of the investments and cash that the fund has and divide it by the number of units in the fund. That fund price will go up and down depending on the changing value of the investments in the fund.

Your money joins with all of the other investors who have also invested, thereby allowing the fund to purchase a diversified portfolio of investments depending on the type of fund you choose.

If it is a stock fund, for example, your money now owns a piece of all of the individual stocks held by the fund. This could range from the shares in fifty different companies to hundreds of different stocks. If it is a bond fund, you share in the income from the range of bonds in the portfolio of the fund. A dividend fund will invest in companies that historically pay their profits out in dividends, giving the individual owners of the fund a share of that income depending on how much you have invested.

A growth fund concentrates on stocks that are focused on growth where whatever they earn tends to be reinvested for the company to develop further. Funds allow you to participate for a strategy, like emerging markets. You could also chose a fund that invests in a particular country only, such as a Canadian, U.K. or Japan fund. Your fund could invest only in a certain commodity, such as gold.

Balanced funds include different combinations of stocks, bonds and cash to give a good return while minimizing the risk. A simple kind of fund is a money market fund that includes conservative interest investments – an ideal solution for parking short-term money that you might need quickly.

Mutual funds also have the benefit of the use of a fund manager. This could be an individual or a team of investment advisers who together make the decisions of what investments to make and when. High net worth individuals who wish to have their money professionally managed use investment advisers. Most people building their portfolio cannot afford the fees to have this kind of expert advice on their investments. By being part of a mutual fund, you can benefit from the investment advisers who work for the fund.

There are a wide range of mutual funds out there, including funds offered through your bank. Work with your investment adviser to select the right fund or funds that match your goals and time frames.

# COURAGE

There are times in life when we have to take a stand against the crowd. In our teenage years, we call it peer pressure. We sympathize with those teens who feel the stress of not conforming to what the popular or persuasive people in their group are doing. To act differently or to stand out is to risk being excluded, laughed at, or worse. Most of us have had the tug of that peer pressure that sometimes seems too strong to fight.

Conformity is not always a bad thing. We are glad when people stop at a red light and drive on the correct side of the road. If no one conformed to the rules, many people would die.

We also know that there are times when the majority can be terribly wrong. Slavery, persecution, religious hatred, and class warfare can all be examples of the powerful or the majority doing harm to others.

It took courage for people to take a stand against the powerful or the majority throughout history. That courage sometimes included social stigma, and sometimes it meant suffering and even death for being true to one's principles.

The kind of courage in the world of finance is not anywhere near that dramatic or important. However, if you are making decisions with your money, it is good to understand how much peer pressure there is to follow the wild swings in what the majority are doing. In the financial world, we call these "bubbles." The one thing you know about a bubble is that it will not last. It might slowly fade until it disappears. Often, a bubble will burst suddenly.

That is great fun if you have been blowing bubbles in the backyard with the children. That is not such good news if you have invested in a bubble.

Bubbles develop when an area of investment gains strength. There can often be good, solid reasons why an area of stocks or real estate is moving higher. Growth does not equal a bubble. What makes growth turn into a bubble is something more subtle. It is what is called "sentiment."

We usually use the word "sentiment" to refer to someone having warm or special feelings about someone or something in his or her past. The sentimental person almost reaches back into that memory or time as if it were real.

A great movie that represented this kind of charm was *Somewhere in Time*, starring Jane Seymour and Christopher Reeve. A 1970s playwright, played by Reeve, wants to go back in time to the early 1900s, when a young actress played by Seymour was a star on the stage in America. The story is set at the Grand Hotel on Mackinaw Island in Michigan. His desire is fierce, and his sentiment is strong. (I will let you find out the rest of the story by recommending it as a good movie for the sentimental audience.)

When this kind of sentiment – a powerful emotion – takes hold of investors, the market becomes "irrational." What was a good idea for investment becomes a great idea, and then becomes a must-have investment no matter how much the price has gone up. More and more investors rush to invest in what seems like a no-lose proposition. All sorts of promoters and pundits will start to say that there is more upside to come. It becomes a sure thing to clean up, with great results just waiting to happen.

Bubbles can develop over months and sometimes more than a year. Something happens where people become certain about something that by definition cannot be certain – the future value of a growth investment. Like a gold rush, everyone is pouring whatever he or she can find into that sure thing: property, stock or precious metal.

Warnings of exuberance are ignored. Anyone who cautions people against in the rush are discounted as disappointed or uninformed.

Then it happens.

# BURST!

The sure thing suddenly takes a big loss. But the mood has not really changed. It is explained as some "profit taking" or a normal correction before the next big move upward. Many put even more into this new bargain opportunity.

Then it happens again.

Kaboom!

A larger and more damaging loss rips the side of your portfolio and like the Titanic – the unthinkable has happened. The ship is going down, and not everyone will survive it financially. The greed of the bubble has claimed more victims.

An upward trending time is called a bull market. A downward trending period is known as a bear market. It is said that bulls can make money and bears can make money, but pigs get slaughtered. There are different strategies that you employ, depending on the trend. But if you get greedy, instead of bringing home the bacon, you become the bacon.

It takes courage to do some of the most basic things that careful investors must do. That means buying when prices are down and selling when prices are up. (As the corny statement says, "Buy sheep and sell deer…")

The challenge is that when investments are down, the majority of people will tell you that it is a bad time to invest. When investments are up, others will tell you to hang on or buy more.

It will take courage to do the opposite of what the crowd is doing. This is where helpful and wise advisers will help you to make the solid choices when they need to be made.

Peer pressure does not end with high school graduation – it just becomes more sophisticated.

Have courage.

# WHEN THEY COME KNOCKING

Whether you are rich or poor or somewhere in between, it will not take long for you to be approached to give or donate to this cause or that one. Many of these groups are very sophisticated in their strategies to target the most likely donors with a message and presentation that will move you to give. Often, it includes a very emotional appeal to get you to give more and to give now.

You might enjoy meeting with someone who is coming to your door asking for a donation. You might be the person on the other extreme who has a sign on his door to discourage any knocks. Some people even hide behind the curtain, checking out the prospector at the door and shushing children and dogs from giving away their tactical position.

There is nothing wrong with this, but as in all of our transactions, we need to know who is buying and who is selling.

Selling is not a bad thing. It is what introduces us to opportunities for something new and different. It may also encourage our support for things we already understand and that have earned our commitment. Without a sale, the economy would stop. Sales are a positive part of a healthy economy.

When you are asked to make a donation to a charity, foundation, educational institution or some other good cause, you need to have the same kind of consumer smarts that you do when you make any purchase.

It is normal for a charity to ask for your support. Most charities do not exist through anonymous benefactors who suddenly appear with a huge cheque. Donations come from people who are connected to the vision created the organization of doing good - whether it was religious, community-based, national or international in focus.

Support for a charity or other institution not only keeps it alive, but is one way to validate whether it is serving the purposes for which it was created.

So how do you evaluate the many organizations that come knocking every year? Which should you support? How much should you give?

Some of the answers to these questions are very personal. Charities or other organizations asking for your support may represent a mission or purpose that is very important to you. They may reflect your values and beliefs in what is important to you. Perhaps a request from an organization researching a particular disease touches you because you have a loved one or friend who died of that condition. If your university calls for your support, you will connect that request to the experiences you had while you were there as a student. These are all important parts of the process for you.

But there are some objective standards that you should apply to your decision, as well. Can you confirm the identity of the organization? Can you give through a cheque (or online) where you know for certain that the cash will reach the organization? Do you receive a receipt to confirm your gift (and that might be part of your tax planning) was received? Can you review a financial statement of the organization? What percentage of your donation will actually go to help those it is intended to help? If the cost of administration and fundraising is above 15%, you might want to ask some questions.

The most important point is to treat your donation as an investment. Ask the question, "How will my investment of my hard-earned money make a difference?" Can my gift be matched by my employer or in some other program to promote giving? Does this organization deserve my support more than others who are asking you for help? Realize that even the richest person cannot solve every need by himself or herself. You can say, "No," to a request because you already have other "Yes" projects that have a higher significance to you. That "No" does not mean that their work is not worthwhile; it just does not connect with you at this point.

As discussed in our S-S-S chapter, sharing is an important balancing principle for your life. When you share, be sure that you are investing it somewhere that will multiply the benefits to your community or in some other corner of the globe where it is needed.

# HUMBLE PIE

The longer you live, the more opportunities you will have for success and for failure. Some of your successes may come down to great decisions you made. Often, it is because we were in the right place at the right time with the right people. It is part of what I teach the children: "Good things happen when you do good things." That is a good general proposition.

Industry, creativity, risk-taking, and especially serving others are often rewarded in this life. Sometimes, however, it does not work out like that. Many people endure difficult times that were not a result of their choices. As the Bible says, "The rain falls on the just and the unjust." (Whether that is a blessing or a curse depends on whether you need the rain at the time, I suppose…) We all know of Rabbi Kushner's great book, *When Bad Things Happen to Good People*. The reverse is also true. We can see many people prosper who seem to live their lives only for themselves.

Just as we should be a bit reluctant to celebrate our triumphs too enthusiastically, we need to keep our failures in perspective, as well. Our successes are built on the gifts given to us by our parents, family, community, schooling, colleagues and customers. Anyone claiming to be a "self-made" man or woman has a problem seeing the world as it is. That does not discount the hard work, persistence and other qualities that helped us achieve the results. But only a fool believes that he was the only author of his success.

Along the way, we also get our share of humble pie to experience. Through bad choices or not paying attention or overestimating our success, most of us will have chapters in our story that are not pleasant at all. These disappointments and failures can be a very positive source of personal growth and development once we find our way to the other side of the experience. But at the time, it can hurt. It can really hurt.

Do not be afraid of failure. That does not mean that we celebrate our failures, but they can sometimes keep us from making important decisions with an even greater loss. These failures can crush our spirit so that we will not make the extra effort next time.

This is where it is useful to read or watch biographies. Many of the great people of our time and distant past went through many uncertainties and even disasters before they could experience success. That is why we need not despair when times are tough. It is not the end of the story – especially when our disappointment is in the area of money.

When you make financial decisions that pay off well, enjoy them. Be careful not to let them go to your head or your heart, however. It is inevitable that all of us will make financial mistakes along the way. Hopefully, through good planning and with great advice, those mistakes will be smaller rather than big ones. Whatever goes wrong, try to minimize the damage.

Then, do not be afraid to have a nice slice of that humble pie.

# IT'S ONLY MONEY

The scenes of the Great Crash of 1929 include people who had been wiped out in the stock market jumping out of buildings to their death.

Financial pressures can poison relationships and lead to divorce and depression. A once promising life seems like it has been reduced to ashes. Chronic unemployment or underemployment can rob someone of his or her sense of self-worth and personal dignity. Financial failure is full of social stigma and changed relationships.

The temptation is to see a bankruptcy or business failure as a final statement of who we are as people. Sadly, many despair and make choices that ruin their futures and those of the ones they love.

I hope that one of the perspectives you have gleaned from this book is that money is a tool we use in our life. It is inconvenient to go through financial difficulties. It is uncomfortable to face a financial failure. But true to most things in life, we can learn more from our failures than from our successes. The dark times give us a perspective on what and who is truly important in life. What you learn is that "It is only money."

Create a list of what is best in life. Like most people, you probably include your family, friendships, health, time and joy in living as treasures not to be wasted.

There is no doubt that money can make many things easier. It is good to work and to try to have your money work well for you.

Rich or poor, there are values that put money in its proper perspective. These are not new. Down through the ages, wisdom literature has warned us about the folly of seeking riches and being consumed by a love of money. Money is described as being part of a trap that captures many people who lose sight of what really makes life truly great.

The truth is that money is morally neutral. It can be used for good or for bad purposes. It is a great servant but a horrible master. How we understand money will affect our relationships, too. If we value money above other qualities, we will miss out on many relationships with people who are not as wealthy as we are (or imagine that we will be) but who would enrich our lives in ways that many wealthy people could or would not.

When we stop to think about it, it is quite obvious. There are wonderful wealthy people along with some hideous ones. There are great people who are part of that phantom middle class along with some middle-class people who are to be avoided. Some poor people are truly rich in what life is about, and some are pathetic.

If we choose our relationships by aspiring to be with those with the greatest bank accounts, we will miss out on those who may not be great but are good. There is a reason why over the centuries there have been references to "the great and the good," since many who are great are not good and many who are good are not great.

So if you face tough times or even financial collapse, keep your perspective. Many of the most successful people financially have endured bankruptcies and business failures. They did not give up. They understood that what was most important was not their bank account. They kept close to the people they loved, followed their dreams, and pursued their passions because that is what gives life energy.

Remember, it is only money.

# A PLATINUM RETIREMENT

Retirement is a topic under review in many cultures. The assumption that we would work for twenty-five or thirty years and then sit on our front porch enjoying the sunset is much more unlikely for most people. What is worse, some people may find that the pension and benefits they assumed would always be there for them no longer can be trusted due to the bankruptcies of companies and even communities.

A bigger question surrounds the idea of retirement. Why retire?

That does not mean that you should or even could keep the same job that you have done in your adult life. However, the assumption that once I reach 55 or 65 I should no longer be employed needs to be reexamined.

As we are living longer, many people who retire at 55 or 60 have the prospect of being retired as long as they worked after graduation from university. The increased life span has also meant more decades of health and vitality. Watch an old black-and-white movie from the 1940s and see how people who reach 60 are depicted. They are typically old, tired and at the end of life's journey. That was true for most, as people usually died around the age of 65 back then. The kind of social security that was created in the 1930s was intended for those who lived past their working age of 65 so that they would not be needy in their final years.

Now that people are routinely living into their 80s and 90s, people at age 65 do not look or act old. Most are people with energy and interest who continue to make a contribution to society wherever they are.

The demographics of Western societies are facing difficult choices when it comes to retirement benefits and social security. The fact that more and more people who were baby boomers are reaching the traditional retirement age means that new fractures in funding government retirement plans are imminent. There are not enough younger workers to fund the cost of the retirees. That would have been true if our life span had not changed, with most people dying in their late sixties and early seventies. We now have not only more people retiring, but many of these new retirees will be collecting their government cheques for 20-30 years. This is a big problem.

Courageous governments (the few) are leveling with their people. Solutions such as raising the retirement benefit age or means testing to determine who needs the support are just beginning to be discussed. The fierce opposition from well-organized seniors groups opposes any changes even if they apply only to people currently in their 40s or 50s. Since seniors are a reliable voting block, politicians are reluctant to do anything that might cost them those precious votes in an election. The result is to do nothing now, with the hope that someone else will tackle it down the road. Mañana.

Related to this are the challenges for companies and governments to properly fund the often generous retirement packages promised to their employees.

Once again, the corporate executives negotiated with their unions on the basis of solving it later. Pension income promised, along with the many benefits, became known as "legacy costs," which described the long-term obligations that were waiting to be paid over the years ahead. Those legacy costs crippled the U.S.- and Canadian-based automobile companies. They were unable to compete with international challengers who did not have those back-end payments to make. That led to a flurry of bankruptcies in the automotive, airline and other big union businesses as the only way to regain a competitive position in the marketplace. Suddenly, all of the retirees who expected the income and benefits promised were facing a less golden retirement.

Cities and other levels of government are facing similar challenges. With reduced income from taxes, a new focus is on the generous retirement benefits structured for workers who can walk away from their jobs while in their 50s with the expectation that they will be comfortable for life. This was a deal that most citizens did not notice or care about when they expected a similar retirement experience. Now that the private sector has shifted dramatically from the highly paid unskilled workers to reduced pay and benefits for the same work, government retirement plans have undergone new scrutiny.

The other challenge is called "double dipping," in which someone completes his required years of service and begins his pension life, only to return to serve the same or similar organization with a new contract or other salary. People are paid to be retired and are still continuing their work. This points out the irrational system that "retires" people in their 50s while they are still productive enough to continue their work for a couple of decades or more.

Ultimately, retirement will have to connect to the person's inability to continue to do the work. Retirement benefits will need to kick in when one is actually retired.

These big changes will not happen quickly or without huge battles between the stakeholders. But the math cannot be avoided for long.

Perhaps as important as planning for these changes, people who retire early without a productive life after work tend not to live as long or as well as those who find purpose in their lives. That may involve continuing or finding a new job that connects to their changing interests or passions in retirement. For many, it is a new focus on volunteering or serving others with their new flexibility.

Instead of seeing retirement as the golden treasure chest to unlock, perhaps it is more valuable to continue to be as engaged and productive a working person for as long as you can in your current job or something new. We often talk about quality of life when it comes to our final years. Of course, the quality of our life should be on our agenda at each stage of our youth, middle age and senior years. The people who finish well usually have a combination of meaningful relationships, a positive perspective on their story and a continuing interest in every day as a new adventure to be embraced.

Sadly, many people see their golden years as a time to switch off much of who and what they have been all their life. They end up moving away from the relationships and opportunities that made them the interesting people they had been over their many years. The "retirement date" becomes a finish line that once crossed becomes an end of more than just their job. The end of work becomes an end of a meaningful existence.

While a particular "job" may end for us, it is important that we never end our career – no matter what our age is. That career may change with the challenges of aging but those who choose to stay engaged with others avoid tarnishing their golden years by becoming self-centered.

As you meet seniors who have chosen to stay involved with engaging and serving others, you recognize that they are much happier and more content with life than those who withdraw into their retirement bubble. The human need to be productive and contribute to our world is not something that stops at 55 or 65.

If you have the opportunity to continue to be involved with some form of work, service or creative activities in addition to your family and friends, you will find your retirement years not as a finish line but a continuation of a life well lived.  That sense of a meaningful life will change how you will approach every day you have in front of you.  Then you will not just have settled for the idea of your golden years, you will have reached the much more valuable platinum years waiting for you to experience.

Have a platinum retirement.

# CONTINUING EDUCATION

For many generations, life was about learning the trade of your father or mother and then continuing that trade. This was usually done in the same community where you were born. It became your life's work.

Now more and more people will have a wide range of jobs over the course of their career. Many types of jobs have disappeared, replaced by technology or workers elsewhere who will work for less money in the global market.

While the temptation may be to blame government or big business for these changes or uncertainties, owning your future requires that you take charge of where you are going.

One of the best insurance policies against unemployment is to be someone who knows how to learn, continues to learn and is willing to change.

Knowing "how to learn" means that you can capture the ideas and skills necessary to do a particular job. That does not mean that you can or should do any or every job. The jobs that connect with our talents, experience and passions are best. But many different jobs can connect with the same skills and experiences that we have.

"Continuing to learn" keeps you fresh and ready to learn something related to a particular job or to have your learning skills ready to take on a new challenge.

Just as any of our skill sets can become rusty, our ability to learn can also become more challenging the longer it has been since we have been in a classroom, studied a book or taken a course online. All of these experiences keep us fresh. This is true of taking in a lecture on something totally unrelated to work. Going to learn about art or music or history all helps us to be stimulated in those parts of our brain in which learning happens. If you attend a religious activity such as a church service, these experiences in which you listen to someone teach or as you enter into discussions all help keep your brain working.

Just as we need to keep exercising our bodies, the discipline and energy required to keep our brain in shape will help us be available to meet the requirements of our workplace.

Another way of thinking about this is to imagine yourself on a highway. If you are travelling at the speed limit, you are "up to speed" and able to navigate the traffic and lane changes as needed. One of the most dangerous parts of highway driving is when you come onto the highway. The on-ramp is designed to get you up to speed before you enter the traffic. If you do not accelerate quickly enough, you may not be able to enter the ongoing lanes of traffic before your on-ramp lane is done.

You may be required to take on new responsibilities in your work. Your job may change within the company, and you may need to learn a host of new skills. You may leave your company and need to take on a different challenge. People who have kept up their learning skills are better able to adapt to those changes that are becoming more commonplace in our competitive world today. It also becomes an advantage on your resume. Employers recognize that people who are hungry to learn will be better able to succeed in the workplace. It can help you get that next promotion or that new job if you need it.

Be a lifelong learner!

That will add wealth to your career and your life every year.

# MULTIPLY

So what have you learned?

Congratulations on reading this book and reading others like it. You have begun your journey toward being an informed investor. You now have the perspectives you will need to truly build wealth in a planned and sustainable way.

When you first looked at the title of this book or began reading it, perhaps you thought this would be a book about being able to "own" more things – to be rich. We trust that as you have explored the concepts that we have developed, you have seen that anything we "own" is merely temporary. What we do "own" is the choices we make. Do not be afraid to build a better future by owning the decisions you make today. Be optimistic about your future.

Take the opportunities you have to take charge of your life. When your choices work out well, be humble. When you make mistakes as we all will do, own them and move on. If you are in one of those waiting periods in life, be persistent. Most of all, own your story. Recognize that you are building it every day, page by page. Make it a story worth telling by having an impact for good in your family, in your career and in your community. You really can make a difference.

We hope that this book has freed you of some of your fears and misconceptions about the choices we all can make with our lives. Those choices are far more important than the ones we might make about a particular investment strategy or real estate purchase. Like so many things in life, when you begin to think clearly, the choices you make later will be better ones.

But do not forget that we also stressed how important the emotional side of money matters is. That is why you need to make choices that are based on your values and aspirations so that you are not a victim of the latest stampede off of a nearby financial cliff. The courage you will need to have comes from believing in the quality of your choices. The best choices are made with wise counsellors there to support and challenge you to ensure that you have it right.

Continue to have a long-term approach. That is tough in the roller coaster ride that some market cycles (or even days!) might include.

Many people spend their life adding. But why add when you can choose to multiply?

Whatever we do for ourselves is addition. That is not all bad. As numbers grow ever larger, adding can be a great thing. Adding bigger numbers gives you a larger result. People who chase money for security or prestige or happiness spend a great deal of their life trying to accumulate more and more. It is as if someone told them that they could never be truly satisfied with yesterday and today – they need tomorrow, too. Too late in life, many of the people who have spent their lives adding end their lives discovering that money cannot buy real security, that prestige is fleeting and that as the old saying says, "Money cannot buy happiness."

We recommend a different equation. Serving the best interests of others is a way to multiply your wealth. Having an open heart and an open hand toward others will give you the unexpected bonus of a positive life.

Positive people are more secure, are truly valued by others, and find the peace and joy of a meaningful life.

We wish you a life that multiplies all that is wonderful so that at the end of your story, you will not just say, "What a Wonderful World," but also, "It's a Wonderful Life!"

# USEFUL LINKS AND CONTACTS

Strategic Seminars - Workshops and seminars for corporations and groups covering topics on business, health, leadership, motivation, relationships, team building, customer service, and more. We are flexible to help corporations and groups of all sizes and with different budgets. There is a special focus on leadership and group development services for corporations. Seminars are offered in the U.S., Canada and the Caribbean. Contact us in Chicago, Detroit or Toronto.
**www.strategic-seminars.com**

Canadian Executive Coaching - Executive coaching for Canadian senior executives, managers, department heads, top salespeople and leaders. Serving a wide range of industry, government and not-for-profit entities with one-on-one coaching to improve performance and provide personal support and reflection. Based on a whole-person model that recognizes our different skills, passions and abilities, Canadian Executive Coaching will help you reach your full potential as a leader and as a person. Member of the Fellowship of Executive Coaches.
**www.canadian-executive-coaching.com**

Harcote Industries – Harcote provides marketing, consulting and distribution services for corporations. There is a special interest and expertise in assisting start-up ventures.
**www.harcote.com**

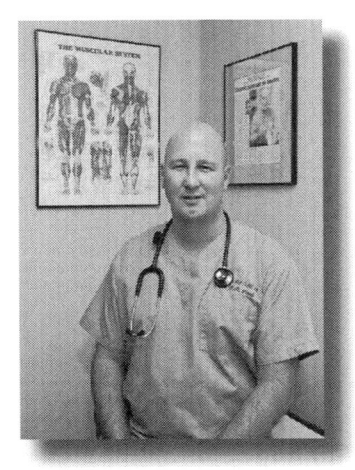

Dr. Blair Lamb, M.D. – The Lamb Clinic is a research and treatment center for the understanding and treatment of pain conditions affecting people of all ages. It has a special focus on fibromyalgia, migraines, arthritis, whiplash, and more. Extensive articles are included on a range of pain topics.
**www.drlamb.com**

Learn about featured seminar speaker Dr. Larry Komer, M.D., with his innovative research and treatments using hormone therapy as part of an overall wellness and anti-aging strategy for men, women and those who have been injured. Excellent information is available on the website for women, covering such topics as menopause, bio-identical hormone therapies, breast cancer and more. For men, you can learn about andropause, testosterone, fitness and the various conditions affecting men. New understanding on traumatic brain injury is part of his research, as well.
**www.drkomer.com**
**www.mastersmensclinic.com.**

Palantir Publishing is the publisher of Grant D. Fairley's Look Up – Way Up! The Friendly Giant. This book is the biography of television's beloved The Friendly Giant – Robert M. Homme.

**www.palantir-publishing.com**

Silverwoods Publishing is the publisher of the book *Up to the Cottage – Memories of Muskoka*, which describes the joys and memories of simple cottages in the golden era of Muskoka. Grant D. Fairley recalls the heartwarming stories typical of life at cottages in the second half of the 20th Century. Whether you spent time in Muskoka, Haliburton, the Kawarthas or another place where cottages and cabins were your home away from home, this book is for you.

**www.silverwoods-publishing.com**

York Downs Pharmacy – Toronto-based pharmacy with advanced compounding as well as other educational and health products and services shipping across Canada.

**www.yorkdownsrx.com**

# ABOUT THE AUTHORS

**Michael H. Lanthier** is passionate about investing.

From his first paycheque, he had the inspiration and guidance of his father to ensure that he would understand the world of finance and grow his money in the future.

Michael is a graduate of Seneca College in Toronto with majors in Marketing and Information Technology.

Like his father, Michael is an entrepreneur and master salesperson, serving and selling to some of the world's largest corporations.

He is a key investor and advisor to a number of start-up and innovative projects around the world.

Michael and his wife Michelle live in Ontario, Canada.

You can contact Michael at michael.lanthier@harcote.com

**G****rant D. Fairley** is a principal speaker with Strategic Seminars, a division of McK Consulting Inc. His seminars cover a wide range of topics, including leadership, finance, team building, sales training, relationships, personal development, motivation, and more.

He is also an executive coach working with corporate and government leaders and senior sales professionals to enhance and develop their careers and personal effectiveness.

Grant is a graduate of Wheaton College, Wheaton, Illinois.

Over the years, he has had a liberal arts life with a range of activities that include teaching, writing and encouraging as common threads in the many roles.

His recent books include *Look Up – Way Up! The Friendly Giant*, the biography of Robert Homme, and *Up to the Cottage – Memories of Muskoka*, a book about the love of old cottages and cottage life in the 1900s.

His book for executives and other leaders entitled, *Positive Influence - How to Lead Your World* from his work as an executive coach. His upcoming book on his unique perspectives on the classic fairy tales and fables is *Enchanted Living - Insights for Your Life from Fairy Tales & Fables*.

In addition to writing books, he is the co-author of a number of patents relating to technology and healthcare.

Most days, he is sharing with others through seminars, workshops and retreats. Some of his seminars are available on YouTube www.youtube.com/strategicseminar. You can hear his podcast chats online about his business and life seminar topics on the BlogTalk Radio channel www.blogtalkradio.com/strategic-seminars

Grant serves as an executive coach providing support and perspectives to senior executives in business, government, sales and other organizations. His podcast chats online about executive coaching on the BlogTalk Radio channel www.blogtalkradio.com/vip-coach

He is especially delighted to serve in his local church.

He continues to learn and grow through his relationship with his wife Cari, the children, the family and friends who are in his story. For these gifts and so much more, he is very grateful.

Grant would welcome your comments on the book and your recollections about your cottage memories. You may contact him at fairley@silverwoods-publishing.com

Follow Grant on Twitter @grantfairley www.twitter.com/grantfairley

His Tumblr blog is called Ship to Shore under the pen name of one of his ancestors, Admiral Wood http://admiralwood.tumblr.com

For more pictures, visit the website www.silverwoods-publishing.com

Silverwoods
Publishing